THE STARVING ARTIST'S WAY

THE STARVING ARTIST'S WAY

Easy Projects for Low-Budget Living

NAVA LUBELSKI

THREE RIVERS PRESS

NEW YORK

Published by Three Rivers Press, New York, New York.
Member of the Crown Publishing Group, a division of Random House, Inc.
www.crownpublishing.com

THREE RIVERS PRESS and the Tugboat design are registered trademarks of Random House, Inc.

Printed in the United States of America

Design by Kay Schuckhart/Blond on Pond

Library of Congress Cataloging-in-Publication Data
Lubelski, Nava.
The starving artist's way: easy projects for low-budget living / Nava Lubelski.—1st ed.
Includes bibliographical references.   1.   Handicraft.   2.   Low-budget cookery.
I.   Title.
TT157.L73   2004
640—dc22   2004012420

ISBN 1-4000-5191-6

10 9 8 7 6 5 4 3 2 1

First Edition

To Steve

Acknowledgments

Thanks to the following:

All of the wonderful artists I mention in this book for (I hope) not being too annoyed at the cavalier way that I refer to you and your work. It is meant to be fun and not disrespectful.

Everyone who generously shared projects, and whose names are mentioned accordingly in the text, as well as to the many who offered great suggestions that I did not manage to include.

Daniel Greenberg, my agent, for flipping the switch that turned me from someone with an idea into someone with the opportunity to write that idea into a book.

Carrie Thornton, my editor, for guiding me through the process of becoming an author, Dan Rembert for the cover, Lauren Dong and Kay Schuckart for the design, Mark McCauslin and Alison Forner for shepherding the book through production, and everyone else at Three Rivers who contributed their efforts to this publication.

Katy Chevigny, Meg Fry, and Ed Sien for plodding through a draft of my manuscript and providing me with insightful criticism, as well as Jesse Levin and Heidi Johnson for sharing your impressions about the visual stuff.

Julia Greenberg for early encouragement in making this project happen, Jeremy Chatzky for help with the endorphin high, Joanna Allman for your generous support, Judah Grunstein for being willing to spend hours discussing everything, even while being so far away.

My fellow former wage-slaves in the G.S. salt mines for making tolerable the intolerable prospect of earning a living while simultaneously trying to be an artist and write a book, particularly the cool cats of the 14th floor, and including A. J. Nieves, whose name I long ago promised to put somewhere in this book in return for his putting up with my yapping all day long.

The brilliant girls of P.S. 3, wherever you may be now, from whom I first learned about collaboration and who joined me in the earliest and most ambitious of wild projects in the interests of fun and worldwide glory.

Stephen Barnard for your essential contribution to the framework of this book and for your continued encouragement and feedback.

My exceptionally creative family: Mom, Dad, Samara.

The incomparable Molly Lubelski, whose acutely motivating pride in the fact of my name appearing on the cover of an actual book, despite everything that was and almost was, is as tangible to me as if you were somehow still materially present.

Contents

The Starving Artist's Way
Making Your World a Work of Art

I t's possible you have this book in your hands and are wondering to yourself: "Just what the #%$ is the Starving Artist's Way, anyway?"

Everyone has heard of the proverbial Starving Artist who struggles to make ends meet, forgoing food to buy canvas and painting masterpieces by candlelight. Starving Artists and their ways of living existed well before I decided to write a book on the subject. On the other hand, the nature of the Starving Artist's Way is to adapt and evolve. The way of the Starving Artist, in these early years of the third millennium, looks different and *is* different from the lifestyle of artists in decades past. The look and feel of a Starving Artist's life today is informed by the ideas that recent art movements and pop culture trends have added to the mix and is reflective of what is current and cool now. The Starving Artist is no longer the guy in the black beret smoking endless cigarettes at the corner table.

Artists have always starved in the name of art, but Starving Artists have continually managed to turn their humble hovels and garrets into artistic realms by using ingenuity to make their surroundings spectacular on a shoestring budget. Being a Starving Artist (S.A.) is a way of life, not a temporary economic inconvenience. The S.A. experiences the maximum in every situation, and even when feeling flush, sips to the dregs to enjoy every last sensation. The S.A. has fun trans-forming what others see as junk—and eventually becoming successful or having some money doesn't change that. The S.A. is always ready to take advantage of life's opportunities for infusing creative style into the humdrum. The S.A. pays attention to the details and to sen-sory inspiration, but without falling prey to the money pits of brand names or the dreary sameness of massive superstores.

The Starving Artist likes to make meals and furnishings at home, but is too hip for Martha Stewart and her cronies. While Martha might grill pricey tuna chunks in the mansion with her guest chef and a bevy of food stylists, the Starving Artist hangs in a funky, skylit loft and whips up a cheap and easy, thrillingly spicy, canned tuna curry while having energy to spare for lots of laughs. While Martha might sew goofy, braided floor mats of store-bought "rags" in her suburban mansion, the Starving Artist hooks a cool-as-hell Pop Art rug out of old grocery-store plastic bags in an outrageously decorated former tenement or converted garage. The S.A. favors cheap, quick, creative ideas with a downtown, do-it-yourself attitude, a no-skills-necessary, quick approach, a budget of small change, and a tremendous amount of artistic imagination.

The Starving Artist differs from other craftsters, like your Aunt Fran who keeps making that same "kitty-cat and yarn ball" needle-point, in more than just aesthetic sensibility. The goal of the Starving Artist is not to make a great centerpiece for that once-a-year dinner party in order to amaze guests but, rather, to genuinely make the most of what is available—to turn nothing into something. Starving Artists transform their very homes and neighborhoods with a desire to live a magical and creative existence, to make new rules and ex-periment with new ideas.

The Starving Artist of any neighborhood loves ideas that are both highbrow and lowbrow at once, which is the tone of the projects you will see in this book. The concept and the workmanship may be unique and clever, but the raw materials could be something as ordinary and ubiquitous as the next-door neighbor's heap of empty egg cartons. The S.A. understands not only that money is saved by making a coffee table from an old door on the street, but also how art theories and trends inform the tastes of the popular culture, bringing Pop Art, Op Art, Ab Ex, Arte Povera, and other modern art movements back into the everyday life that originally inspired them.

The decision to write this book grew out of the realization that not everyone knows how to live like a Starving Artist—that is, how to live inexpensively and yet maintain the attitude that your own life is the richest experience that could be. I realized that not everyone knows how to cook like an artist—not even all artists can do it, in fact—it is defined by a particular ability to be in the moment, take risks, trust instincts, "change the plan" in response to unexpected results, and remain determined to pull off something great no matter what. I first thought about writing this book when I realized that not everyone has friends who whip up amazing inventions and innovations to suit any situation, friends who feed you with style even when they're broke or give you awesome presents when they didn't know until five minutes ago that it was your birthday.

I thought about writing this book when painter Jessica Dickinson showed me the quirky, subdivided bedroom she jerry-rigged from the scrapped lids of packing crates. I thought about writing this book when I saw the ultra-stylish kitchen counters that painter Chris Hopewell built cheaply from plumber's pipe and plywood. I thought about writing this book when poet Chad Davidson made a spur-of-the-moment dessert of granita from the leftover breakfast coffee. I thought about writing this book when I watched video artist Theo Angell brew absinthe and then, completely sober, start filming the movement of the liquid in the jar because it looked so cool. I thought about writing this book when collage artist Kathy Bruce, in an act of creative stealth that made me laugh out loud, mailed me a package containing the "food people" we'd made out of cheese cubes and olives one late night after an opening a full year previously—who else would take the risk or the trouble? I thought about writing this book the time Jason McKay lassoed a terrifyingly trespassing rat with a homemade catching device constructed in a flash of rope threaded through a short length of pipe. Meanwhile, I stood by with my hands in the air, still mouthing the word *rat* silently to myself. Everywhere I turn I see artists inventing furniture, games, and food; solving practical problems with an infusion of inspiration; and making life richer without spending an extra penny.

I don't mean to romanticize poverty here—extra cash is downright useful and I'm willing to admit it. But with clever ideas, you can turn a tight budget into an exciting challenge and have a good time figuring out how to outwit even your own cravings for more and bigger stuff to cram into your life. If you have nothing, try thinking of your environment as "Minimalist" (see page 89). If you are overwhelmed by clutter, think "assemblage" (see page 190). An unexpected spill might be viewed as a bold act of "Abstract Expressionism" (see page 74) or a repetitive task made amusing by being tagged "Actionism" (see page 220).

In writing this book, I have peppered the project descriptions liberally with references to artists and art movements whenever they occurred to me. Some of the associations between a particular project and the artist mentioned are tenuous at best, but I make no apologies. Finding art in unexpected places, while not taking it too seriously, is part of the game; and as I go, I explain something about the artists and genres I mention for those readers who don't recognize the references. Dropping a few interesting names has always been part of the Starving Artist's Way, and it will encourage you in the attitude of entertaining yourself with art in any and every situation. The word *attitude* is no accident here, referring as it does to the too-cool-for-school persona that artists may often appear to project, and is just part and parcel of having a good time.

Some of the one hundred projects in this book are weirder and wackier than others. Creating felt from cat hair or coasters from bubble gum is obviously not for everyone, while Coffee Granita and Spaghetti Carbonara are recipes that can be found in all sorts of ordinary cookbooks. The Starving Artist's Way is not all nutty or all normal—it is a collection of far-out, appealing, or interesting suggestions, some of which I'm sure you'll want to try out and others of which you'll just have a good time reading about and then steer clear of. Some of the projects are original inventions and some are culled or adapted from other artists, but all have a sensibility in common. They are relatively easy and made of basic materials and ingredients, but they all have a spark of something funky and spontaneous that is the essence of the Starving Artist's Way.

The idea for this book came naturally to me as I started on the Starving Artist's Way at an early age. I grew up in a loft in the 1970s pre-boomtown of New York's SoHo. The space that my family called home was a cavernous industrial floor of an old building, originally designed for light industry, that could accommodate my father's painting studio, as well as our living quarters. With the help of a few friends, my parents put in the necessary walls, plumbing, and wiring to make a home.

The kids of our neighborhood went Dumpster diving among the leftovers on the factory back streets, dragging home bundles of colorful electrical wires for sculpting, fabric remnants for sewing, and strange, vaguely mechanical-looking objects for "inventing." It is only in retrospect that I notice we had no parks or playgrounds nearby—back then I hardly noticed. We just made stuff all the time and felt pretty lucky about it.

In the early 1990s, I moved to Williamsburg, Brooklyn, the "new bohemia" first so labeled in a *New York* magazine article at that time. My roommates and I found a loft in a building that had stood empty for ten years, abandoned by the knitting factory that had formerly occupied its premises. Sewing machine needles still glinted from the cracks in the floorboards and the knitwear packaging stashed in the stairwell made great wallpaper. The building was sandwiched between a plumbing-parts retail business and a warehouse for a bagel-making equipment distributor. As in the SoHo of my childhood, the workers and pickup vans cleared out after dark and the neighborhood was deserted. I was quickly able to recognize the handful of other artists dotting the landscape and holing up in the nearby buildings. A plant and the glow of indirect lighting in the upper-floor window of a dingy factory was a dead giveaway.

Times have changed in the New York hoods of Williamsburg and SoHo, artists eventually making way for anyone who could afford the skyrocketing rents, but new neighborhoods continue the tradition. Homesteading and pioneering continue in America today, and the new frontier consists of Starving Artists laying claim to urban areas abandoned by industry or considered undesirable for a host of other reasons, transforming public and private spaces and creating new neighborhoods. Eventually the neighborhoods become so desirable that most artists are forced to move on to fresher, cheaper spots. This is the story told not only by New York's SoHo in the 70s and Williamsburg in the 90s, but also famously by Chicago's Wicker Park and the Mission District in San Francisco. It continues to be told all over the country in neighborhoods like the Warehouse District and Northeast in Minneapolis, Chicago's Bucktown, Seattle's Belltown. Across the globe, urban neighborhoods have seen the same type of transformation, from Kreuzberg and Prenzlauer Berg in Berlin to Bastille in Paris. Furthermore, while I'm a born and raised city-dweller, I know that Starving Artists can be found all over the place—in small towns, in suburbs, and in cabins in the woods, staking a claim wherever they happen to be.

The important essence of the Starving Artist's Way is that you can be poor and not really know it. If you have something unique and beautiful, that nobody else has, you'll feel well-satisfied. This will also cause you to stop complaining so much, making life better for everybody else and thus increasing the general morale of the planet.

So to sum up: the basic tenets of living like a Starving Artist are, wherever you may find yourself:

- Make it yourself
- Make it cheap
- Make it cool

Food

Food is a good thing. That said, everyone has his or her own idea of what makes a great meal and we don't always agree. For example, you may be forgiven for asking why most of the recipes in this book are meatless. The answer is simple: politics aside, vegetarian eats are generally cheaper, quicker, and less suspect fresh-wise. There are some exceptions: my pal Katy Chevigny's Carbonara recipe is as cheap and fast as they come, and I included it because she complained to me that I needed to make sure to feed the carnivores, too. Let me be clear, though: while the Starving Artist's Way of eating is not pot roast with frozen peas and carrots, it's also not some kind of hippie thing, with big pots of brown rice slopped drearily into clunky and misshapen bowls. *Au contraire*, everything needs not only to be inexpensive and easy but also to have a sparkly or unusual edge. For that reason, the Starving Artist avoids traditional entrées and instead goes for a selection of soups, salads, appetizers, and comfort courses. With a dazzling array you can shirk the idea of a big and time-consuming main dish. The point is to stimulate your senses and even your mind, and leave everyone satisfied (and not simply in the same old grilled cheese or rice and beans kind of way, tasty as those things might be).

Included here are also some special ideas for entertaining within a budget, whipping up treats to surprise impromptu guests, and all-around tips for acquiring a reputation as being unflaggingly interesting and full of surprises (in a nice way, though, something well short of doing a "pig out and puke" **Patty Chang** tribute at the dinner table).

There are endlessly daring possibilities in the history of creative entertaining that might not appear on the Style Network, but deserve props for contributing to the spirit of budget living. I don't want to advocate breaking the law in the interests of hosting a posh dinner party, but you have to admire the inventiveness of this one: Abbie Hoffman, in his manifesto on revolutionary activity and living on the cheap, *Steal This Book*, has a remarkably inexpensive recipe for what he calls Hedonist's Deluxe. The recipe begins, "Steal two lobsters, watching out for the claw thingies," and continues with a fairly straightforward description of boiling the lobsters and dunking the cooked meat in melted butter. To obtain the butter, in order to reduce the cost of the meal still further, it is recommended you use what Hoffman refers to as "the switcheroo method," swapping the contents of a margarine package in the supermarket with four sticks of the (obviously more expensive) butter.

> **Patty Chang**
> American performance and video artist (b. 1972) who pushes the limits of good taste in videos like *Stage Fright*, where, in a bathroom stall via a live TV feed, she continually eats and vomits. In others she goes even further—for example, appearing to drink water off the floor of a public men's room.

Some Suggestions for Eating Well the S.A. Way

- Notice color (it is no accident that a recipe including red pepper with green vegetables and yellow spices makes for a colorful dish).

- Use garnishes (i.e., chopped parsley, cilantro, or chives added at the end) for aroma and to fancy-up your presentation.

- If you don't have vinegar, any acid can work well in a salad dressing. Try squeezing a fresh lemon or orange. Or use a splash of Tropicana, in a pinch.

- Get a pepper grinder if you don't already have one. This will cost only a few bucks and is a crucial quality-of-life enhancer. Freshly milled pepper is much more potent than the pre-ground, already gone-stale, sawdusty kind in the shaker, and it is packed with vitamin C, so it may save you money in the long run on supplements and cold medicines and flu shots and tissues and woolen long johns. I'm the world's biggest cheapskate, and there's not a lot I'd recommend plunking down money for, but I would always plunk some for a pepper grinder. Of course, they hawk fresh pepper all over the Food Network, too, so this is not exactly a radical suggestion.

- A point about carbohydrates: If you don't want your tasty dish on a bed of rice, you can always serve curries and stir-fries over a bed of shredded lettuce or lightly cooked, shredded cabbage. These are lighter and very healthy alternatives to rice or pasta, and still give you something to fill up on.

- Make dessert when you are having people over. This *is* possible to do affordably, and otherwise you may disappoint your guests. Your friends should be dazzled after a visit to your home, and sugar does wonders to seal the deal. Anyway, do I really need to pitch the idea of *dessert* to anyone?

- Keep your olive oil in an empty wine bottle. It saves money because you can buy bigger containers and decant. Also, it looks kind of European, pro chef-like, and you can't put a price on that.

- Keep it interesting: You may not have endless funds to pay your filet mignon bill, but you still shouldn't be eating the same thing every day. If all you ate were one meal over and over, you'd probably get scurvy or some other oddball sailor's illness. At any rate, a lack of variety gets dull, and dull is not by any means the Starving Artist's Way.

- Enjoy the great artistic tradition of using what you have. Take a tip from the master: One of the classic artist recipes of all time is Andy Warhol's *A & P Surprise*—two-day-old sponge cake soaked for 36 hours in ½ cup rum. Now that does sound yummy.

Comfort Courses

The idea behind the "comfort course" is of a dish that can be made easily and cheaply, but provides a hot and filling update of a classic favorite. These can be one dish meals, with just a salad on the side, and they are generally based on the easy-to-make, satisfying, and cheap classic sides like pasta or rice, though included here are some tips for avoiding high-carb content, if that's your bag.

WONDER BREAD PIEROGI

In the Williamsburg-Greenpoint neighborhood of Brooklyn, a community that's recently been made world famous by its population of artists and hipsters, there are a plethora of Polish diners serving hearty pierogi breakfasts to the hungover and inexpensive pierogi dinners to the hard-up. Greenpoint was and is primarily a Polish neighborhood, and like many trendy urban enclaves, it originally attracted both immigrants and artist with its low rents.

Of course the pierogi you get at a diner is made from a traditional Polish recipe. The Starving Artist, however, does not have time to be kneading pierogi dough and has adapted the tools of modern living to the creation of delectable pierogi at home. Remember as a kid when you used to take your slices of bread and mush them and roll them up into little balls? Well, here's an adult way of playing with and recrafting your food to make a creative and tasty dinner on the fly (the combination of childhood behavior and Polish culture is one that Polish artist **Zbigniew Libera** used to effect in his contro-

Zbigniew Libera Polish contemporary artist (b. 1959). Most famous for his controversial "shock" art of Lego concentration camps replete with guards, barbed wire, and skeletal inmates, he also served time in a Polish prison for making drawings considered pornographic by the then-Communist government. Much of his work reflects on consumerism, in the form of toys and other products.

versial Lego pieces). The filling can be many things, but try this classic Polish favorite: mushroom and sauerkraut.

WHAT YOU'LL NEED FOR A SINGLE PORTION

Olive oil or butter, for cooking
1 garlic clove, chopped
1/4 cup finely chopped mushrooms
1/2 cup sauerkraut, drained
salt and pepper
4–5 slices sandwich bread
1/4 cup sliced onion
Lemon juice, maple syrup, chopped chives;
   or applesauce and sour cream, for serving

Sauté the garlic and mushrooms for a few minutes over medium heat to soften the mushrooms, but avoid burning the garlic. Mix with the sauerkraut and season with salt (if necessary—your brand of sauerkraut may be salty already) and pepper.

Take a slice of bread and place on your cutting board. Cut off the crusts and gently press the center of the slice to compact it, leaving a spongy margin of about ½ inch all around. Enjoy the sensation of playing with your food. Put a tablespoon of filling into this pressed area. Lightly moisten the edge of the slice by dipping your fingertips in water and running them over the ½-inch border. Fold the slice in half, encompassing the filling and pressing around the dampened edge with your fingertips to seal it shut. Make the remaining pierogi in the same manner.

Heat a large pan to medium-high with more oil or butter, then toast the pierogi on both sides until lightly browned. Fry the sliced onion (you can do this while cooking the pierogi in the other half of the pan) and serve pierogi topped with several onion slices. Drizzle with a dressing of one part lemon juice to one part maple syrup and chopped chives or the traditional applesauce and sour cream.

Don't forget to use the cut-off crusts of the bread for croutons (cut into bits, toss with olive oil, salt, and pepper, and bake in a hot oven for 10 minutes until crunchy). The Starving Artist wastes nothing.

PEANUT BUTTER CURRY CONSPIRACY

Peanut butter curry is one of the Starving Artist's best tricks of the trade. The **"conspiracy"** referred to in the title is a glorious culinary secret, actually unrelated to 1960s psychedelic rock. This dish can be whipped up in moments and tastes rich, satisfying, and delicious. It's exotic and comforting at the same time, although if you get to thinking about **William Pope.L.** and what he did with peanut butter, you won't feel as relaxed, so maybe wait until after dinner for talking art. This recipe is for a vegetarian version of the curry, as peanut butter is luxurious and decadent enough without meat, but you can adapt the recipe to include your choice of *carne,* if you so desire.

Peanut Butter Conspiracy Los Angeles–based psychedelic band that formed in 1966 and whose first LP was *The Peanut Butter Conspiracy is Spreading.* They lasted only a couple of years and never really managed to step out of the shadow of the massively more famous band of the same genre, Jefferson Airplane.

William Pope.L. American performance artist (b. 1955). A professor at Bates College in Maine, he painted a lynching out of Skippy peanut butter, as well as creating many other works out of food such as Pop-Tarts and hot dogs. In performances he has eaten a copy of the *Wall Street Journal* and crawled through crowded streets in a Superman suit.

Curries are generally made with a blend of spices, commonly turmeric, cumin, and coriander, sometimes cinnamon, mustard, and others. This unconventional recipe for peanut curry includes yellow prepared mustard from the jar (this ingredient comes courtesy of musician Stephen Barnard—also check out his risotto recipe later in this book). The yellow pigment in mustards is turmeric, which is also the main ingredient in curry. Mustard contains some additional, generally unspecified, curry spices (like mustard seed itself) as well as vinegar, so it's a quick way to add curry flavors to this dish without having to stock a huge array of ground spices.

You can use any brand of peanut butter that you have—they all work. Some are pre-sweetened, and if you use that kind don't add any other sweetener to the dish. If you use sugar-free peanut butter, you'll want to include the honey from the ingredient list.

Cook some rice if you want it. You can do this according to the directions your mother gave you, or the ones on the package. On the other hand, this is an example of a recipe you could serve over shredded lettuce or cabbage just as easily and avoid the extra starch, so prepare a heap of lettuce if you want to go that route. Then, prepare your ingredients.

YOU'LL NEED

1/2 onion, diced

2–3 garlic cloves, chopped

2–3 teaspoons chopped fresh ginger

1 tablespoon olive or sesame oil

1 red bell pepper, diced

2 cups chopped broccoli

10–12 mushrooms, chopped

1 zucchini, chopped

1–2 carrots, chopped

1 cup peanut butter (I prefer crunchy)

1/4 cup soy sauce

1/4 cup yellow mustard

Hot sauce to taste

1/4 cup honey (you won't need this if you use a sweetened
    brand of peanut butter)

1/4 cup water, or as needed

1/4 cup chopped cilantro

1/4 cup chopped scallion

Sauté the onion, garlic, and ginger in the oil in a hot pan until all are coated and the onion is beginning to brown. Stir in the vegetables, cover the pan, and turn the heat down to medium. Give the contents a stir every minute or so and then re-cover while you prepare the sauce.

Combine the peanut butter, soy sauce, mustard, hot sauce, and honey and whisk together. Stir this mixture into the pan of vegetables, add as much of the water as you need to make the mixture stirrable, and turn the heat down to low. Leave uncovered while it simmers for about 5 minutes, stirring occasionally. Add more water if the sauce gets too thick. Check the broccoli for doneness and then remove from heat. Garnish with cilantro and scallion.

This will serve 4 to 6 people, depending on how hungry or greedy they are. While eating a peanut butter meal, discussion should flit around the subject of the aforementioned artists, as well as **Wim Schippers** and his peanut butter carpet. Food for the mind as well as the body . . .

> **Wim T. Schippers**   Dutch Fluxus artist (b. 1942). He created a
> 16-square-meter peanut butter carpet. Though well-known in his native
> Europe in the 1960s as an artist, he later became a host and writer for
> children's television, ultimately remembered by most as the voice of
> Ernie in the Dutch-language version of *Sesame Street*.

THAI TUNA

There is one grand secret to Thai cooking, a cuisine that while seemingly exotic can be captured pretty accurately if you only know the code words, *fish sauce*. That's all. Anything you've got— any vegetables, any meat, any starch—will magically become a Thai meal with this addition. Fish sauce is sold in Chinatowns and Asian markets all over the country. Go get a bottle now, and it will last you forever, as you use only a splash at a time. If you can't find it, though, the Starving Artist can offer the following alternative:

Fish sauce is made from anchovies, sugar, salt, and water. Anybody can get anchovies, as they are a cross-cultural condiment and they come in little cans and bottles available in any supermarket. To make your own fish sauce, you'll want to mash or blend a 2-ounce can of anchovies with a teaspoonful of sugar (or honey) and ½ cup water. Since these canned anchovies are not live fish you needn't worry that you'll find yourself in a Danish courtroom, though anyway **Peter Meyer** got let off in the end. Anchovies are generally pre-salted, which is part of the point of fish sauce, so don't be alarmed by the salty, fishy taste of this liquid. It smells pretty fishy, too, but you won't smell it once it's been added to the other ingredients. You can keep this homemade fish sauce for quite a while in the refrigerator, and a couple of tablespoons at a time will do the trick.

Canned tuna is the way to go for a cheap at-home feast. You can serve it over salad, rice, or just straight up. You can swap out the vegetables to your own taste, though it's best to have a combination of bright colors or it won't look as good (and as a result, won't taste as good, if you follow my logic). The fresh cilantro just makes this dish de-licious-er and Thai-er, but if you can't find it, so be it—you might try fresh basil instead, also a favorite component in Thai cooking, or even fresh parsley, if need be. Just don't forget the fish sauce.

Peter Meyer Danish director of the Trapholt Museum in Kolding, Denmark, who was charged with animal cruelty for showing a piece in the year 2000 by Chilean-born Danish artist **Marco Evaristti.** Live goldfish were presented in blenders that the audience was permitted to turn on, should they choose. Someone did and charges of animal cruelty were brought against the museum. A Danish court ruled that the fish were likely killed instantly and "humanely," and ruled in favor of the defendant.

YOU'LL NEED

Cooking oil, such as olive, sesame, or peanut

1 small onion, chopped

1 6-ounce can tuna, drained

1 teaspoon finely chopped fresh ginger

1 garlic clove, chopped

1 red bell pepper, chopped

1 small carrot, chopped

1 cup chopped mushrooms

2 cups chopped any firm green vegetable, such as zucchini,
    broccoli, and/or string beans

2–3 tablespoons fish sauce

Several sprigs cilantro

1 lemon, quartered

Begin with a hot pan and your choice of cooking oil. Cook the onion for a minute or two to brown and then add the tuna. Toss these together and continue to cook for a minute before adding the ginger, garlic, and vegetables. Cover the pan for 2 or 3 minutes. The lid will allow the vegetables to cook in their own moisture. Stir the pan, add the fish sauce, and re-cover for another 2 to 3 minutes. Check the vegetables—they should be firm, but tender enough to eat. Turn off the heat, toss in the cilantro sprigs, and serve immediately over your choice of rice or salad with lemon quarters. What a lovely Still-life with Fish. **Braque** would be proud.

    Serves about 4.

Georges Braque   French Cubist painter (1882–1963). Along with Picasso, Braque is credited as the creator of Synthetic Cubism, and during the beginning stages of the style it's pretty hard to tell their work apart. Braque frequently incorporated actual collage into his paintings and was fond of Frenchy-looking still lifes with newspapers and fishes and bottles of wine.

"OCTOPUS PROJECT" FRIED RICE

This dish can feed quantities of people cheaply, and it provides a little extra unexpected something—namely, that touch of octopus. As Japanese artist **Shimabuku** said about his *Octopus Projects*, "Art must be magic, very cheap but very good." Yep, that sounds like a Starving Artist's mantra. And it definitely sounds like a Starving Artist's meal.

Goya sells octopus in a can, and a couple of those cans are all you need to make something different out of the same old pot of rice. (Goya, in this case, refers to the distributor of Latin-cuisine canned goods and not the Spanish painter **Francisco Goya**.) This dish is also designed to be made when you're stuck without any fresh vegetables; it was invented late at night when the only store open near my apartment was the corner deli, and I was almost entirely limited to what they had to offer—that is, foods that keep for extremely long periods of time on shelves. This recipe is also a good way to use up leftover rice. Try it out; it tastes good and did I mention that it has *octopus* in it?

> **Shimabuku** Japanese installation artist (b. 1969) whose interest in process-based works led him to spend a couple of years traveling in search of a mermaid and to take a live octopus on a tour of Tokyo. He was in search of answers to questions like "Would the octopus be pleased at receiving the gift of a trip to Tokyo? Or would it be annoyed?"

You'll need a quantity of cooked rice for this dish, depending on how many people you'd like to feed, but once again, a note about carbs: You can always replace rice with shredded cabbage. In this case, you just swap the cooked rice for raw cabbage, and as you stir-fry, the cabbage will cook.

YOU'LL NEED

Olive oil

1 medium onion, chopped

2 garlic cloves, chopped

1 10-ounce package frozen peas

4 cups cooked rice

2 4-ounce cans chopped octopus (plain or in garlic sauce)

2–3 scallions, chopped

1 medium tomato, chopped

Paprika, cayenne or hot sauce, salt and pepper

Several sprigs cilantro or parsley

Heat a large pan on medium-high, and in 2 tablespoons olive oil, cook the onion and garlic for a minute or two to get them started. Stir in the frozen peas and give them just a moment to thaw before adding the rice and octopus. Stir and cook for a couple of minutes to warm everything. Stir in the chopped scallions, tomato, and 1 teaspoon paprika and ½ teaspoon cayenne or a few dashes of hot sauce. Add salt and pepper to taste. Continue cooking and stir to mix thoroughly. Add the chopped fresh herbs, adjust seasonings as needed, and serve very hot.

Serves 4 to 5.

Francisco Goya

Spanish Romantic painter (1746–1828) who painted Spanish royalty and also some rather uncharacteristically macabre subject matter for his time. Of course, his famously gory "black paintings" are now thought by some experts to have been painted by someone else, probably his own son or grandson. Most of his paintings, real or otherwise, are housed in the Prado museum in Madrid.

CARBONARA WITH SPINACH

Documentary filmmaker Katy Chevigny gave me this recipe, one she learned from her mother, who apparently learned it from a bunch of firemen when she was a starving grad student. (I know that sounds like a made-up sitcom situation, but my understanding of the story is that Katy's mom just happened to live next door to the firehouse.) This is incredibly fast to make (appropriate for firemen who, like artists, never know when duty will call) and doesn't require much in the way of fussing around. It sort of cooks itself after you prepare all the ingredients, which is about all you could ask from a dinner recipe.

Again, the carbonara can be tossed with gently cooked vegetables instead of spaghetti, if that's your preference. In this case, you might try a panful of chopped and sautéed zucchini, peppers, and yellow squash.

YOU'LL NEED

1 pound bacon, cut into 2-inch pieces

3 large onions, sliced

2 eggs

Grated Parmesan cheese

Freshly ground pepper

1½ pounds spaghetti

1 pound fresh spinach

Bring home the bacon and fry it up in a pan. Seriously, do it. Stir often so it cooks evenly. When the bacon begins to pucker from frying, add the sliced onions, stirring frequently. Cook until bacon is done and onions are caramelized.

In a big serving bowl, crack the eggs and whisk them together. Then whisk in enough grated cheese for the egg and cheese mixture to thicken into little peaks in the bowl. Grind lots of pepper into the sauce so that it will be peppery and delicious.

Boil the spaghetti. Right before the spaghetti is done, heat up the bacon and onions, then using a slotted spoon to drain the grease, add the bacon and onions to the cheese-egg mixture in the bowl. Stir quickly together to cook the egg.

Pour off most of the bacon grease from the pan into a disposable dish or jar (feel free to find some resourceful use for it if you don't want to throw it away—believe it or not, **Ed Ruscha** did silk-screening with bacon grease and spinach—you've got all the ingredients at your fingertips), and quickly sauté the spinach in the pan. It will look like you have mountains of spinach, but the mound will quickly cook down to a manageable amount. Drain the spaghetti, and add the spinach and the spaghetti to the bowl. Toss to mix the sauce evenly over the pasta. Serve with extra pepper and cheese on the side.

This dish will feed around 4 people cheaply.

Ed Ruscha   American Pop Art painter (b. 1937) (pronounced roo-SHAY) who became prominent for pieces that played with texts as symbols, images and ideas of Americana and lots of stenciling, incorporating such unconventional materials as gunpowder, chocolate, spinach, and bacon grease.

MAC 'N CHEESE PUTTANESCA

No, there's nothing tawdry about this dish; don't be fooled by the name, which in Italian supposedly means something about prostitutes. And no, even though this may sound to you like a macaroni dish that's fit for a cheap whore, you won't end up, **Gauguin**-like, dropping off from syphilis. At least not from eating this dish—take care as you go about the rest of your life. The name's just a rip-off of the tomato-based puttanesca sauce that is usually served on spaghetti and resembling a catch-all of little bits of different tastes.

Paul Gauguin French Synthetic Symbolist painter (1848–1903) who is most well known for painting numerous scenes of half-naked women lounging around in Tahiti. He was a stockbroker into his mid-30s before leaving his day job to spend some time with (crazy Vincent) van Gogh at Arles, though apparently the two did not get along too swimmingly.

YOU'LL NEED

1 pound macaroni
2 tablespoons olive oil
1 red bell pepper, diced
1/2 cup diced onion
2 garlic cloves
1 teaspoon red pepper flakes
2 tablespoons Dijon mustard (or your personal favorite)
1/4 cup chopped green olives

1/2 cup chopped tomato
1/2 cup chopped parsley
3 cups grated cheeses (Cheddar or any combination
   that you like)

Cook the pasta just the way they say to do it on the box. Luckily pasta always comes with instructions in case you've forgotten.

Meanwhile, heat a pan to medium-high, put in the olive oil, bell pepper, onion, garlic, and hot pepper flakes and sauté until the onion begins to turn translucent, a few minutes. Turn off the heat and stir in the mustard, olives, tomato, parsley, and cheese. Stir in the drained pasta. Mix quickly.

You can bake this in a glass or ceramic dish, or even a bread tin, for 10 to 15 minutes in a 350 degree oven with a drizzle of olive oil and a sprinkle of cheese on the top. You can also dispense with the baking; just give it a toss, and serve it while the pasta's still warm. This dish is easy and tasty, and I'm totally fine with you telling people you made up the recipe yourself.

Serves around 4 people, depending somewhat on degree of hunger.

AVOCADO-MUSHROOM RISOTTO

Musician/composer Stephen Barnard invented this simplified and fresh summer risotto for feeding a big group. Like the perennial favorite pesto, this dish is fresh and fragrant and satisfying without requiring too much stove time or endless stirring of hot broth into rice, as with the more traditional risottos. Finding ways to twist an old classic into something experimental is the very essence of the Starving Artist's Way. The use of mushrooms here is a particularly artistic touch, as it brings to mind those **Roxy Paine** hyper-real mushroom sculptures. You can host a mushroom-drawing contest in conjunction with serving this dish, which is a fun party game as anybody can draw something approximating a mushroom, whether he or she has any artistic skills or not. See my accompanying mushroom drawings for inspiration.

> **Roxy Paine** American conceptual artist (b. 1966) who has created various repetitive "painting machines," as well as numerous, extremely realistic models of psychoactive mushrooms and of poppies.

As for the ingredients, arborio rice is traditional for risotto and has a creamy quality, but this does not mean you have to use it. At the risk of sounding like a perky kid on an episode of *Zoom*, I would recommend trying it once in order to compare it to other types of rice and then see what suits you best. Trial-and-error, playful experimentation is as essential to the Starving Artist's Way as it is to the National Science Foundation's encouragement of young minds through educational and upbeat TV programming.

YOU'LL NEED

2 cups rice

2–3 tablespoons olive oil

Salt and pepper

1 small onion, chopped

8–10 mushrooms, sliced

3–4 garlic cloves

1 small jalapeño pepper

2 avocados

1 juicy tomato

1 tablespoon grated fresh ginger

Several sprigs chopped cilantro

Grated Parmesan cheese (optional)

Cook the rice according to the directions. (If you use arborio rice for this and are feeling lazy, you can cook it as you would any other rice, in spite of the risotto instructions on the package, which means 2:1 water to rice, bring to boil, and lower to a simmer until cooked. The texture will be slightly different from usual risotto, but no biggie.)

Meanwhile, sauté the onion and mushrooms in olive oil over medium-high heat with some salt and pepper until they brown a bit. Set this aside and prepare the sauce. In a blender, chop the garlic and jalapeño, add the avocados and tomato, a couple tablespoons olive oil, the ginger, and cilantro. Add salt and pepper to taste and blend the whole thing to an orangey sauce.

When the rice is almost cooked, toss in the mushrooms and stir. Continue cooking until the moisture is entirely incorporated into the rice. Take off the heat and add the avocado mixture, stirring to incorporate all the ingredients. Taste for salt. Garnish with some more chopped cilantro and grated Parmesan if you like.

Serves 2 to 4.

Soups, Sides, and Appetizers

INSTANT JAPANESE SOUP

This is a soup for those got-nothing-in-the-house moments when you are just about dying for something warm and tasty. At the same time, it's extremely classy and subtle in that Japanese way and not a big goofy mess like the slop people often associate with healthy cooking. It also provides a convenient moment to reflect on some of Japan's contemporary artists. I can't promise that it's as funky/quirky as a big eyeball by **Takashi Murakami** or a video by **Mariko Mori,** but it's edible (unlike those works of art), so it shines within its own parameters.

Sadly, I can't remember the name of the woman who showed me this dish, but she

Takashi Murakami Japanese contemporary sculptor and painter (b. 1962) best known for his brightly colored giant pop eyeballs and Mr. DOB, a mouselike character he created in the style of Japanese anime.

Mariko Mori Japanese performance and video artist (b. 1967). The glamorous Mori dresses up (à la Cindy Sherman) as various characters of her own creation. The result is a continually morphing sci-fi fantasy with Mori personifying an eternally mesmerizing, futuristic Pop princess in an environment of kitsch and 3-D stylishness.

was a friend's roommate, and what I do remember about her is that she had bright orangey-red hair and almost burned the house down with a candle placed unfortunately close to a curtain while she was making this soup. There should be no danger involved in the preparation of this meal, but keep an eye on your candles, at the very least. That's good advice no matter what you are working on.

YOU'LL NEED

1 1/2 cups water

1 tablespoon tamari or soy sauce (this is the key ingredient, which flavors the broth and provides saltiness)

1 teaspoon olive or sesame oil

1 scallion, finely chopped

1 teaspoon grated fresh ginger

Leaves from 5–6 sprigs parsley, watercress, or cilantro

7–8 small cubes firm tofu, or 1/4 6-ounce can tuna, or a couple of sardines, mashed

1/2 cup cooked rice, rice noodles, or soba noodles

Freshly ground pepper

Dash of Tabasco or any other hot sauce, if you like it spicy

Put the water on to boil, put everything else in a bowl, toss it around once, and when the water boils, just pour it over the top. Presto.

Serves 1. Double or quadruple the above recipe for guests, roommates, or family members.

PRESERVED LEMON WITH MOROCCAN SALAD

Preserved lemon is the sort of salad add-in that could guarantee one's reputation as a true Starving Artist forever. It is both exotic and refined, but not pricey, giving you that **Paul Bowles** expat-in-North Africa kind of vibe. Make this condiment when you have a spare 10 minutes. It will be ready within 5 or 6 days, though best in about a month (it basically has to pickle) and will keep refrigerated for about half a year. This gives any salad that sumptuous Mediterranean flair, and will make you feel like you've jumped into one of those beautifully colored **Matisse**-in-Morocco paintings. Use it in cooked dishes, too.

Paul Bowles American writer and composer (1910–1999) known for such novels as *The Sheltering Sky*, which was adapted into a film by Bernardo Bertolucci. Bowles wrote consistently about human alienation, and is something of a legendary cult figure because he lived most of his life in Tangier, where he partied with the Beat poets whenever they came to visit. He was married to Jane Bowles, though they both seem to have maintained continuous and open homosexual affairs.

Henri Matisse French Fauvist painter (1869–1954) and one of the most influential artists of the twentieth century, Matisse is considered a bridge between Impressionism and Expressionism. Known for his celebrations of color, flat shape, and pattern, Matisse is also responsible for the quote that art should be "a good armchair" (not an idea currently in vogue—these days art is supposed to be "challenging"). He visited Morocco in 1912, and made a large number of paintings and drawings there and afterward, influenced by the brilliant colors and light of the region.

YOU'LL NEED

5 lemons, plus juice of 3–4 additional lemons
1/4 cup salt
1 cinnamon stick
3 whole cloves
5–6 coriander seeds
3–4 black peppercorns
1 bay leaf

Jane Bowles American playwright and novelist (1917–1973) greatly admired by Tennessee Williams and Truman Capote among others, but never quite achieving true literary "fame." Her work is considered subtle and she completed very little, probably owing to health and emotional difficulties (she was institutionalized by her husband, Paul Bowles, from 1967 until her death) and probably too much alcohol consumption. Paul claimed that the publication of Jane's first play *In the Summer House* inspired him to begin writing, and after her death he claimed that he was no longer able to write fiction.

Wash the lemons, quarter them, and sprinkle insides with salt. Put 1 tablespoon of the salt on the bottom of a clean jar, such as a thoroughly rinsed pickle or mayonnaise jar. Put the lemons in the jar, alternating each piece with salt and the spices, and squish them down so the juice runs out. Add the additional lemon juice to cover the lemons in the jar. Leave the jar out for 5 to 6 days, giving it a shake every day. Then put it into the refrigerator. The lemons will get better and better, and will be perfect in about a month. Cut into small pieces for salads. When serving to guests, you might casually mention that you think **Jane Bowles** was a better writer than her husband and vastly underrated among today's readers.

If you need a suggestion about how to use preserved lemon, try a chopped Moroccan Salad. This salad is tasty and quick, and can be a nice variation if you'd like a change from the usual lettuce-based variety. It would also be perfectly healthy to eat it every day for the rest of your life, so feel free to indulge.

YOU'LL NEED
2 cucumbers, cubed
2 medium tomatoes, cubed
1/2 small red onion, finely diced
1/4 cup fresh mint or parsley, chopped coarsely
1/4 cup preserved lemon (see previous recipe)
1/4 cup chopped pitted Greek olives
1/4 cup olive oil
Juice of 1/2 lemon
Salt and pepper

Toss together all the ingredients except the last three. Drizzle the olive oil and lemon juice onto the salad and sprinkle with salt and pepper.

TOSSED DINNER SALAD

If you like your salad to have lettuce in it, try this one. It's got a range of tastes and textures: sweet, salty, cold, warm, soft, and crunchy. An epic, if you will. Speaking of epics, I highly recommend making the attempt to read **Tolstoy**'s *War and Peace* if you haven't already. I managed to get all the way through the classic novel while working an overnight temp job a few years back. (The sort of "day" job that artists of all sorts find themselves taking on for extra cash.) It's startlingly contemporary, and if you skip some of the longer "war" segments, it won't take as long as it would otherwise. Definitely one of those classics worth keeping—hmmm, kind of like salad . . .

Leo Tolstoy   Russian novelist and philosopher (1828–1910), Count Leo Nikolayevich, writer of such hefty tomes as *War and Peace* and *Anna Karenina,* was preoccupied with issues of agrarian reform and other political and philosophical subjects. His books contain a density of plot and an intertwining of such a multitude of characters that they put to shame even the most complex of modern-day soap operas, while still including observations about grass seeds stuck on a cart wheel, the shape of a hand as seen through a skirt pocket, and other equally minute details of daily life. The resulting novels are inevitably and famously long.

YOU'LL NEED
1 head of romaine
A handful of watercress, spinach leaves, or parsley sprigs
1 small apple, chopped
1/2 small onion, chopped
2 tablespoons capers
Salt and pepper
2 tablespoons olive oil, plus a drizzle
1 tablespoon mustard
Juice of 1/2 lemon
1/2 cup coarsely chopped mushrooms
1/4 cup walnuts

Rinse and drain the romaine, then rip it violently and dramatically in half and then in half again. Toss the first five ingredients together in a salad bowl. Sprinkle with salt and pepper. Whisk together the olive oil, mustard, and lemon juice and dress the salad. Sauté the mushrooms in a drizzle of olive oil on high heat for 5 minutes, uncovered. Toast the walnuts in a dry pan over high heat; just shake them around until they start to brown and then pull them immediately off the heat. Toss the nuts and mushrooms into the salad while still warm and serve immediately.

Serves approximately 4 to 6 people, depending on how epic you'd like the experience to be.

SESAME-ENCRUSTED CHEESE HORS D'OEUVRE

This five-minute recipe is a delicious and easy party snack that tastes and looks a lot more spectacular than it is. If you're serving plain old cheese for a party, you might feel obliged to buy fancy and expensive brands

Clara Peeters Flemish Baroque painter (1594–1657) who painted many of what are known as the Dutch "breakfast piece"—still-life arrays of cheeses and herrings.

and blow a lot of money in the process, but there's no need for that. This recipe makes a layout of **Clara Peeters** opulence from the most basic of *fromage* budgets.

YOU'LL NEED

1/4 cup (4 tablespoons) butter

1 cup cubed cheese (a combo of any semi-hard cheeses like Cheddar, Muenster, or Monterey Jack)

1 cup sesame seeds

Black pepper and chopped parsley, for garnish

Take butter and cheese and blend together in a food processor until creamy and fairly uniform. Now, taste it. Notice how the added butter immediately gives the cheese a Brie-like and fattening, expensive quality? (You can add a drop of hot sauce, a few olives, chives, or any other spice or fresh herbs at this point, but it's also fine without anything.) In fact, if you're already running short on time you can just mold the mixture onto a plate and serve as-is with crackers or cut vegetables. Call it **"Erasmus** Cheese Spread" or something like that, while we're on the subject of dead Dutch people.

But, if you have time for a top-notch presentation, continue the recipe: Toast the sesame seeds by putting them in a pan over medium-high heat and shaking around for about a minute until they are lightly browned and beginning to make popping noises. Remove immediately from heat (to avoid blackening) and allow to cool. Make a small ball (about gumball-size) of the cheese mixture and press lightly into cooled sesame seeds, allowing your ball to flatten slightly into a poker-chip shape. Flip over and press again, then roll the edge in the seeds.

> **Desiderius Erasmus**
> Dutch Humanist philosopher (1466–1536) most famous for the book *The Praise of Folly*. He has been noted as making the strikingly profound statement that "he who has cheese does not need dessert."

Stack on a plate and garnish with a touch of black pepper and chopped parsley. These are so damn good that I am almost sorry for telling you about them. Just make sure you save some for your friends and don't finish them all yourself. Self-control is going to have to be your own project.

Makes 10 to 12 hors d'oeuvres.

OLIVE AND BLACK BEAN TAPENADE WITH ROASTED GARLIC

Olives, along with bread and cheese, seem to be traditionally arty food—I guess because people eat them so much in Europe, whence came the original bohemian-style Starving Artists. You can easily picture **Pablo** or one of those other old arty dudes chowing down on just about olive-anything, can't you? Olive tapenade is a delicious treat as an hors d'oeuvre, a breakfast spread, or for any other time

Pablo Picasso
Spanish Cubist painter (1881–1973) who I'm sure you've heard of already. After his "blue period," he painted such classics as the early Cubist *Les Demoiselles d'Avignon* (1907) and his memorial to the Spanish Civil War, *Guernica* (1937).

you want to put something different on bread. Since good olives are pricey, you can make this spread go further if you incorporate some black beans in the mix. This will save money, an obviously crucial concern for the Starving Artist, and will give the dish an edge of **Diego Rivera** Mexican flair.

Diego Rivera
Mexican muralist and Social Realist painter (1886–1957) known for a style that married European "modern" painting with native Mexican art, creating a uniquely Mexican twentieth-century art form. Also known as the philandering husband of Mexican Surrealist painter Frida Kahlo.

First, for the standard version:

IN A FOOD PROCESSOR, MIX

1 cup pitted black Greek olives

2 garlic cloves (raw or roasted—see recipe below—
   depending on your audience)

2 tablespoons olive oil

Freshly ground black pepper

This will yield a nice amount for serving as a party snack or before a dinner party of 6 to 8 people.

IF YOU WANT TO MAKE THE BLACK BEAN VERSION, ADD TO THE ABOVE MIXTURE

1 16-ounce can cooked black beans

2 additional garlic cloves

1 tablespoon olive oil

1/2 cup toasted walnuts (optional)

Chopped parsley or cilantro, for garnish

Put the beans, additional garlic, and extra olive oil with the basic tapenade into the food processor and blend. You can also add ½ cup toasted walnuts. When serving, garnish with chopped parsley or cilantro.

The addition of the beans will give approximately twice the yield of the olive spread alone.

Roasted Garlic

Preheat the oven to 350 degrees. Place a whole head of garlic on a baking sheet, drizzle with olive oil, and bake about 20 minutes or until the top browns. The garlic will be hot, so allow it to cool before you start pulling it apart. You will find that the garlic has turned soft and will be easy to push out of the skins. Also, the bitterness has faded. The garlic puree can be spread on bread as it is or included in many dishes.

RADISH TAPAS

The radish is a particularly beautiful food, with a satiny smooth, carmine red exterior and pristine, white crunchy innards. The radish is a real charmer, and if you like to eat them raw, as they are almost always served, you will be happy ever after. Many people, however, find the radish too bitter or the raw crunchiness too banal for human consumption. Rabbit food, they call it. Gosh, that makes me think of **Cecily Brown**'s bunnies, and it almost starts to sound kind of sexy or something. Anyway, radish-haters need their radishes dolled up a little and the sautéed radish is for them.

Surprisingly, the radish loses its bitterness after just a little bit of cooking. Maybe this is actually *un*-surprising, as it's the same behavior displayed by the onion, the potato, the garlic, and most dark leafy greens. Maybe the real surprise is just that

> **Cecily Brown**
> English contemporary painter (b. 1969) best known for her expressionistic "bunny paintings" that show glimmers of rabbits in sexual acts, almost disguised in a frenzy of brushwork.

most of us walk around assuming the radish to be a raw-only food. At any rate, inveterate radish avoiders will happily eat this:

YOU'LL NEED
1 bunch radishes (probably 8–10 radishes)
2 garlic cloves
Olive oil
Salt, pepper, and paprika
Fresh rosemary, marjoram, or other available herb
    (optional)
Chopped Italian parsley, for garnish

Take the bunch of radishes and slice them into disks. Smash the garlic. Heat 1 tablespoon of olive oil in a saucepan over medium-high heat and put in the radish and garlic along with some salt and pepper. Cook this uncovered, stirring a few times, until the radishes appear lightly browned. Toss with paprika and fresh rosemary or marjoram, and cook for 1 minute more. Remove from heat and put in a serving dish. Sprinkle with chopped parsley for greenness.

This side dish will serve around 4 people.

The idea of "tapas" (a Spanish custom of various small dishes eaten at the bar) is to have some good wine and a few tastes of different flavors. People will say "ooh" and then "ah" when they try this one with some good, fresh bread. Conversation should be peppered with references to any Spanish artist you find interesting. Try **Juan Muñoz** if you need a suggestion.

> Juan Muñoz   Spanish sculptor (1953–2001) whose work generally involved sculptural dwarves, dummies, or other human figures strangely inserted into altered architectural spaces where they more or less just hang around.

BROCCOLI STEM PICKLES

Now, before you freak out about how the stem of the broccoli is so dreary and inedible, let me say this: The biggest mistake you can make with the broccoli stem is to try to pass it off in a stir-fry, along with the flowery parts. People won't be grateful for the chance to bite into the tough, fibrous, bland thing. That said, broccoli stems are basically a delicately flavored underachiever, only great if you encourage them to feel special by keeping them at a distance from the bullying rest of the broccoli floret mob. So, make the flowery bits one day and prepare the stems solo for the next. From the Starving Artist point of view, broccoli stems are also basically free, as they are so often chucked in the trash after the heads have been cut off and cooked. This is a tragic mistake.

Broccoli stems need to be peeled. The outsides and the ends are tough, but once you clear those away you have an unusually versatile vegetable on your hands. These tender insides can be boiled for five minutes and pureed with potatoes as an update on the classic mash, or cubed and sautéed with garlic and salt and pepper for a simple side dish with a lovely geometric presentation that nobody's ever

Tobias Rehberger German installation artist (b. 1966) who creates living works of planted vegetables and herbs, part sculpture, part landscape architecture. The pieces have referenced modern artists, such as Piet Mondrian, in their form. Broccoli, as well as sunflowers, was planted as part of the 2000 installation *The Sun from Above.*

seen before. Or you can make this broccoli pickle, to be served as a condiment with almost any meal or tossed in a salad. Hell, you can make an entire landscape of broccoli and other pretty plants, and call it the latest in German installation art, with inspiration courtesy of **Tobias Rehberger.** But for starters, here's the pickle recipe:

YOU'LL NEED
Stems from 1 head of broccoli
1–2 garlic cloves
Salt and pepper
Lemon juice or vinegar

Peel and cut off the ends of the broccoli stems and cut into small cubes. Toss these cubes into boiling water for no more than a minute to slightly tenderize them, and then transfer them, drained, to a small jar or bowl. Chop the garlic and sprinkle generously with salt and pepper (and any other spices or herbs). Cover the whole business with the lemon juice or vinegar and give it a day to marinate.

Drinks

AT-HOME ABSINTHE

Absinthe is now illegal in much of the world, including the United States, but back when it was freely available it was the original Starving Artist's creative aid. Stories abound of how lots of the old French guys rotted out their brains from hallucinating on absinthe all over Arles, Montparnasse, and various other French locales. **Degas** even has a painting called *The Glass of Absinthe*. In general, selling any homemade alcohol is illegal, but brewing it for personal consumption seems to keep you on the right side of the law and all the ingredients, including the supposedly psychoactive wormwood, are legal herbs. Apparently thujone, a narcotic component of wormwood, can cause major neurological damage when ingested in large quantities and is considered "unsafe for human consumption" by the FDA, so whatever you decide to do, proceed with caution.

Expert absinthe makers insist that you have to use a still to make the real thing. They are probably correct about that, but that also

Edgar Degas
French Impressionist painter (1834–1917) who made it his business to paint a whole lot of ballerinas and who, partly as a result of his sophisticated compositions and partly because of the pretty girls in the pouffy tutus, remains eternally and extremely popular.

raises additional legal issues, as using a still is a federal crime if you don't have a license. Video artist Theo Angell showed me how to make this simple, undistilled absinthe at home, but be warned: Using herbs can be dangerous as they are potent plants used for medicinal purposes—they are not just goofy hippie weeds. I'd advise you to be careful anytime you ingest unfamiliar substances, be they herbs, alcohol, or anything else, and to understand the possible effects they may have on your body. Furthermore, when Theo made this stuff he poured it into Styrofoam cups, and it started dissolving them at a startlingly rapid pace, so I can only imagine the implications for your stomach. To sum up, proceed at your own risk—I'm saying I

Vincent van Gogh Dutch Post-Impressionist painter (1853–1890). The original Starving Artist and source of most of the myths about tortured creative geniuses who are appreciated only after death. Famous for *Starry Night* (1889) and other canvases painted at Arles, France, where he lived and worked his last years, as well as for the fact that he cut off his own ear. Van Gogh wrote lots of letters to his brother, Theo, and spent a considerable amount of time in the company of fellow painter Paul Gauguin, which ultimately doesn't seem to have been that good a time for either of them as Vincent was going nuts and Paul made him feel worse. See Robert Altman's *Vincent & Theo* for more details as well as Tim Roth's personification of the speeding train wreck.

really don't know what this stuff is capable of and apparently **van Gogh** drank a lot of it and look what happened to him. Or hadn't you heard?

Anyway, for safety's sake and legal reasons, I'm going to present here a wormwood-free version of absinthe that has the taste and the look, but not the potential danger. Enjoy!

YOU'LL NEED

1 tablespoon angelica, chopped

1 tablespoon star anise

1 tablespoon fennel seeds

1 tablespoon licorice root, chopped

1 fluid ounce peppermint extract

1 quart vodka, rum, or grain alcohol

Gilbert and George English performance and conceptual artists (Gilbert Proesch b.1943 and George Passmore b.1942). G& G are a pair of dandy-ish English guys who use themselves as their art—in performances, photographs, and video—their very actions becoming the piece itself, be it singing, painting themselves some odd color, or just hanging out, getting drunk, and taking a bunch of pictures.

Put the herbs and extract into a quart mason jar and cover with the alcohol. Put it in a cool, dark place like the back of a cabinet and give it a turn upside down every day. Just let it brew for a couple of weeks. Strain out the herbs before drinking, pressing to remove the alcohol.

Absinthe is traditionally served with some water and a sugar cube. Place the cube of sugar in a spoon, balanced over a glass containing a shot of absinthe. Drizzle water over the cube, dissolving the sugar into the glass.

You'll get around a dozen drinks from this mixture.

If you finally invite people over to drink the stuff, imagine that you are creating a **Gilbert and George** "sculpture" out of your evening. A few photos as the party gets in full swing will give you a close approximation of the G & G (1972–73) piece *Smashed*.

POMEGRANATE JUICE AND POMEGRANATE LIQUEUR

This nectar of the gods is what I serve when I want to wow everybody with a super taste sensation. Pomegranates are usually so hard to eat owing to the seeds and membranes that nobody ever gets the chance to relax and enjoy them fully, and as a result, pomegranate juice feels extremely decadent. It's also rich and delicious, and great to accompany dessert or in place of wine for those who already drank too much last night. Or last year. But you can make a liqueur from it, as well.

Pomegranates have recently been shown to be very good for you, too, and P juice is being marketed as the best antioxidant money can buy. This is super news as anything tasty that can also help avoid future bills for chemotherapy and other nasty medical procedures is a "good thing."

Pomegranates are beautiful, and have made numerous appearances in works of art. **Catherine Wagner** created an entire *Pomegranate Wall*. **Wols**'s *The Blue Pomegranate* is a classic of early European abstract painting, which FYI doesn't look anything like a pomegranate (hence the descriptive label "abstract").

Catherine Wagner American photographer (b. 1943) whose interest in science and institutions led her to create *American Classroom* (1987), a series of photographs of school science experiments. She has also photo'ed freezers full of human genetic material and the cell-like unit of the pomegranate, as in *Pomegranate Wall*, a giant series of MRIs.

Wols German-born French painter (1913–1951) whose work bridges the representational and the abstract with a style that suggests Abstract Expressionism.

You'll need a manual citrus juicer for this recipe, which I recommend getting anyway, as it allows you to juice fresh oranges early in the morning or late at night without waking anybody up with the annoying whirring of motorized appliances. You can buy one inexpensively at a housewares store or even a junk shop, as it's the kind of kitchen tool that's been in circulation for a century or more and people repeatedly buy one, use it for a while, throw it away when they lose interest in making fresh-squeezed juice, and then find themselves with a hankering again.

Eight to ten ripe pomegranates will do you for a quart of juice. Peel the red outer skin off the pomegranates, and separate the chunks, removing the whitish membranes that divide the sections. Put the juicy seeds into your juicer and press down with the handle to squash the juice out. Keep going until you've juiced all your fruit. This process will be messy and take a while, but it will be worth it.

Alternatively, R. W. Knudsen and Lakewood both make a bottled 100 percent pomegranate juice, which will run you anywhere from 3 to 5 bucks for 32 ounces and can be found in many health food stores. If you need something to bring as a gift, or to a dinner party, you can fill a clean, old wine bottle with some store-bought pomegranate juice and give that as a gift without really discussing whether or not you made it yourself. The wine bottle makes the juice as fancy as it ought to be. Tie a ribbon or a product gift tag (see page 228) as a label/card around the neck of the bottle and you will be considered ultra-charming by all and sundry.

TO MAKE POMEGRANATE (OR ANY FRUIT) LIQUEUR:

1 cup sugar

1 cup boiling water

1½ cups pomegranate juice

Pint of vodka

Make a concentrated syrup by dissolving the sugar in boiling water. Allow the syrup to cool. Mix the juice and the vodka in a glass jar, add the sugar syrup, and seal. Let the mixture brew in a dark corner in the sealed jar for a couple of months, shaking it every few days. After brewing is finished, pour off the liquid, and discard the sludge from the bottom of the jar. Filter the sediment from the liqueur and enjoy.

Makes about a quart of liqueur—enough for a very pleasant evening with friends.

TEAS

Tea is a traditionally arty drink, either because it makes you think of soft-spoken anticaffeine 70s Bohos or because so many painters, **Cézanne** included, made still lifes with teapots featured prominently. I have a copy of a particularly funky one by **Vallotton.** And tea's the perfect drink

Paul Cézanne French Post-Impressionist painter (1839–1906) who was really the first Post-Impressionist of them all. He focused on landscapes and still lifes—lots of bowls of fruit—with an eye for articulating geometric form.

for tackling a hefty book on a cold winter's day: you might try **Calvino**
or **Borges** for extra-credit smarty points.

Felix Vallotton   Swiss/French Post-Impressionist painter
(1865—1925) and one of the Nabis, a group that also included Pierre
Bonnard and Edouard Vuillard. Vallotton's style was characterized by
a Gauguin-like interest in flat shapes. He was well-known for his wood-
cuts, influenced by Japanese prints.

Italo Calvino   Cuban-born Italian Post-Modern novelist
(1923–1985) who created works of fiction that expose their own
structure and yet remain eminently readable. For a cold evening's
tea-drinking, try the appropriately titled *If on a winter's night a*
traveler (1979) with its broken, half-sentence, lowercase title as
an example of one of the book's multiple experiments in form.

Jorge Luis Borges   Argentinean Modernist author
(1899–1986) whose examinations of randomness and human search for
meaning often took the form of short stories, such as "Pierre Menard,
Author of the Quixote," the tale of a twentieth-century man who
rewrites *Don Quixote*, word-for-word but better, including in-depth com-
parisons of identical passages of the two texts.

Spicy Ginger Tea

This is a spicy tea that's great in the wintertime. It's highly aromatic and will perk up the senses, an important aspect of the Starving Artist's Way. You can also make it iced for summer. You can use the skins and leftover stumps of ginger if you have them from cooking another dish.

Fill a teapot with about ½ cup thinly sliced fresh ginger and ¼ cup honey. Pour in boiling water and allow the tea to steep for 5 minutes before serving.

This will make 4 to 6 cups.

Mint Tea

A big pot of this tea makes a great after-dinner mellowing-out drink. It is also nice to serve this in the afternoon if people drop by. Fresh mint grows like wildfire if you have a place to plant it; in fact, it's prone to squeeze out all other herbs in your garden. Or you can buy it by the bunch at the supermarket for around a dollar.

This is best served out of a single large teapot and poured into glasses so most of the mint leaves stay behind. Fill the teapot with 2 cups fresh mint leaves and 4 tablespoons sugar. Pour boiling water to fill the pot and allow it to steep for 5 minutes before pouring out. Put a sprig of mint in each glass and provide more sugar for those who want it.

Serves 4 to 6.

Desserts

INSTANT BREAD-N-JAM MINI LAYER CAKES

Uh, oh. Forgot to make the cake? Try this no-bake instant mini layer cake. It's the thought that counts . . . and anyway, it's the icing that makes the cake—everybody knows that. The experience of making these cakes is a bit like bricklaying, so you might think of it as a work of **Socialist Realism,** or better yet, an excerpt from **Wajda**'s *Man of Marble*, which happens to be about a champion bricklayer. It's great, and I suggest you see it, but I am digressing. Let's get back to cake.

Socialist Realism A term coined around the time of WWII to refer to art that attempts to embody the ideals of Socialism. The phrase is mostly used to refer to art coming out of Soviet Russia at that time, or more accurately to art *not* coming out of Soviet Russia at that time. In the West, Diego Rivera (see page 40) is an artist normally associated with Socialist Realism.

Andrzej Wajda

Polish filmmaker (b. 1926) who directed *Ashes and Diamonds* (1958) and *Man of Marble* (1977), and is considered to be arguably the defining Polish filmmaker. His 1981 sequel to *Man of Marble*, called *Man of Iron*, is also the story of the Solidarity movement in Poland and the Gdansk shipyard strikes.

YOU'LL NEED

4 slices ordinary sandwich bread, white or whole wheat

1/2 cup peanut butter (pre-sweetened or add 2 tablespoons
confectioners' sugar), whipped with 1/2 stick
(4 tablespoons) butter and 1 teaspoon vanilla extract;
or 1/2 cup of raspberry jam

2 cups chocolate icing (you can use the store-bought kind
or use the chocolate truffle recipe (on page 65) at room
temperature, with or without the spicy pepper)

Lay out two slices of the bread on your cutting board. Spread one with filling and the other with icing, and lay them face to face. Spread the top of this sandwich with filling, another slice of bread with icing, and lay the new slice facedown on the stack. Again spread the stack with filling, the next slice with icing, and lay it icing down on the stack. Trim off the crusts by cutting down the stack on each of the 4 sides, creating a neat rectangle. Ice the top and sides with the remaining icing. There's your mini cake. Because of its richness it is enough for 2 to 3 people.

As an alternative, you can fill the layers with jam and use the peanut butter mixture as the icing, for a peanut-butter-and-jelly-sandwich cake. You choose.

If you need a bigger cake, you can make four of these mini layer cakes, put them next to each other, and ice across the seams as smoothly as possible. Or just make a row of several identical cakes for a **Wayne Thiebaud** display. You can top the cakes with any of the traditional decorations, or slap some legs on the bottom for a **Laurie Simmons** "walking cake" replica.

> ## Wayne Thiebaud
> American Pop Art/Realist painter (b. 1920). A quintessentially California painter, Thiebaud's most popular works are his paintings of food displays, particularly rows of cakes and pies, created in bright, delicious colors with an eye for geometry and pattern.

> ## Laurie Simmons
> American conceptual photographer (b. 1949) who is particularly known for images of self-created sets and dolls, and for her "walking" series of photographed objects with legs on them.

COFFEE GRANITA

Chad Davidson, poet, contributed this recipe, which was originally shown to him by his friend Vince Verna. Chad and Vince had eaten this over in Italy, where they spent some time being arty and Italian.

This basically costs nothing because you can make it with leftover breakfast coffee, but it provides a touch of glamour at the end of a

Henri de Toulouse-Lautrec French Post-Impressionist painter (1864–1901) who happened also to be a dwarf, a fact which may or may not be relevant artistically, but like most things, probably was. He lived a life of debauchery in Paris, eventually dying of drink. His lithographed posters of girls in frothy can-can skirts remain particularly recognizable.

meal and a bit of the "late night with **Toulouse Lautrec** at the Moulin Rouge" feeling, too. As a matter of fact, unless you have a high tolerance for caffeine, you *will* be up all night after eating this and you'll have to find something to do with yourself. No matter. Most Starving Artists do great work at night, since they don't have to be at their pesky day jobs during the dark hours, or answering calls from the ruthlessly persistent day-time telemarketers. The night is a good time to concentrate. If you aren't feeling productive you can also party till dawn like the Spaniards do, and imagine yourself eating tapas in the shadow of **Gaudí**'s magnificent Sagrada Familia cathedral. On the other hand, **Nietzsche** described coffee as a spreader of darkness and took an extremely negative stand on the subject of coffee consumption, so that's something else to think about when you're lying awake after too much postmeal caffeine.

Friedrich Nietzsche German Existentialist philosopher (1844–1900) who is famously quoted as saying that "God is dead." He ranted and raved and opposed all kinds of stuff including the moral abstraction of Christianity and... drinking coffee, stating unequivocally in *Ecce Homo* that coffee "spreads darkness."

Antoni Gaudí Spanish Art Nouveau architect (1852–1926) whose rounded, malleable-looking buildings are located mostly in the environs of Barcelona and include the Sagrada Familia and the Casa Mila apartments.

Of course, granita is an Italian food, and strangely I'm rapping about everybody under the sun except the Italians. Especially when I should be explaining how to make sinfully delicious Coffee Granita. Here goes:

YOU'LL NEED

4 cups coffee

1/2 cup sugar

Ice cube trays or baking pan

Make or rescue the remainder of a pot of strong, dark roast coffee or espresso and add the ½ cup sugar, or just enough until it tastes sweet enough to be a dessert. Let the coffee cool slightly and pour into ice cube trays and put in the freezer. If you don't have enough ice cube trays, you can pour it into a baking pan and follow the more traditional method, which is to give it a stir with a fork every 15 to 20 minutes. Eventually it will freeze, but the stirring will prevent it from becoming rock-hard and impossible to serve. The Starving Artist method is to leave the cubes to freeze solid while you're busily creating other masterpieces. When you are ready for dessert, put the ice cubes into a sturdy plastic bag and pound them with a hammer or other blunt object (or pulse in a sturdy blender) until they are sufficiently broken up to enjoy.

This will make enough granita to serve 6 to 8 guests.

Dish out a few scoops in a glass or bowl with Sambuca or other liqueur and a dollop of whipped cream or vanilla ice cream. The buzz you get from this could definitely be the thing that kick-starts your next great oeuvre.

GIANT LEMON GUMMY BEARS

This amusing dessert is a cross between Jell-O and enormous gummy bears, and is funny and fun for the whole family. If you want to make this gummy bear, you'll need one or several empty plastic honey bear bottles. (You can just pour the honey into a different jar and rinse the honey bear bottle clean.)

If you don't have a bear mold, you can also make gummies into "jiggle cubes" in an ice cube tray to enhance a dessert of ice cream, chocolates, or cake. Or make a baking tray full of gummy mixture and cut out shapes with a cookie cutter.

This recipe is quick, which is good, or else the combination of unexplained bears and the feeling of being trapped in the kitchen forever might start to remind you of some kind of **Luis Buñuel** nightmarish dinner party.

Luis Buñuel
Spanish Surrealist filmmaker (1900–1983) who incorporated such tricks as having two actresses play the same role in *That Obscure Object of Desire* (1977). Buñuel first made cinematic history when he collaborated with painter Salvador Dalí (see page 217) on the film *Un Chien Andalou* (1929), in which he created the hideous and unfortunately all-too-memorable image of a razorblade slicing through an eyeball.

YOU'LL NEED

Vegetable oil

2 packets (2 tablespoons) unflavored gelatin

3/4 cup water

1/4 cup fresh lemon or other citrus juice (2–3 lemons)

2 cups sugar

Food coloring (optional)

Prepare your bear: with a craft knife, cut the empty bottle down the sides, behind the side seams, leaving the screw-on cap and the ring that holds the cap in place (see drawing). If you can't cut through the bottle all the way around (sometimes the bottoms are thick and hard to get through), cut just the sides, leaving the bear's back connected at the base and work around it. Mutilating the bear will put you in a nice **Mike Kelley** frame of mind and help you to act out some of your domestic-related aggression. If this idea is particularly working for you, then go ahead and de-capitate the bottle and use just the head of the bear for your gummy treat.

Lay the bear mold-face down in a bak-ing pan, nested in a dish towel for balance. (Other possible molds are small rubber duckies sliced in half down their center lines, doll heads, or just an ice cube tray, as mentioned above.) Lightly coat the chosen mold with vegetable oil, so you won't have trouble removing your finished gummy treat.

Mike Kelley American sculptor and video artist (b. 1954). His dissections of dirty, old stuffed animals are his best-recognized pieces, and a photo of his work was used as cover art for Sonic Youth's 1992 album *Dirty*. His video *Heidi* (1992), a macabre remake of the children's tale made with Paul McCarthy, is also considered a classic.

Combine the gelatin with ¼ cup water. Combine the lemon juice, sugar, and remaining ½ cup water in a saucepan over high heat and bring to a boil—if you don't like lemon or sugar, you can use any unsweetened fruit juice for this. Add the gelatin mixture, shut off the heat, and whisk the whole thing for a moment. Make sure your gelatin mixture is not so hot that it can melt the thin edges of your plastic bear. Give it a moment to cool if necessary. Add a few drops of yellow or green food coloring if you want. Pour into molds and refrigerate for several hours.

You can unscrew the bear's cap to loosen him and then nudge him out of the mold onto his flat back. The way the gelatin fills the lip and lid of the bottle will make your bear look like one of those dancing cubs in a Russian circus wearing a bellhop's cap. You may want to cut the hat off with a knife if you require a bear that is completely naked as in the wild. For cubes or other shapes with no screw-off cap to loosen the mold, use a wet butter knife to help you nudge the gummies out. If you have poured the mixture into a plain baking tray, use lightly moistened cookie cutters and just pop the finished gummies onto a plate. Watch it jiggle, see it wiggle.

This recipe will make 1 giant gummy bear, or several smaller gummy shapes.

Note: Agar (aka agar-agar) is a gelatin substitute that is made from seaweed instead of pig hooves. You can use this, and it works well as a general thickener for sauces and to give a pudding-like consistency to liquids. For this project it takes an awful lot of agar to get a firm gummy, and is not so affordable or worth it unless you are much attached to the gummy idea and very unattached to the use of gelatin. Instead of gummies, you can make delicious lemon custard if you add a few tablespoons of agar to the above recipe in place of the gelatin. You'll need to actually boil and then simmer the ingredients for about 5 minutes or until the seaweed breaks down and is dissolved, and then allow the mixture to cool and set up, but you won't get to use the bear mold with this mixture.

PEANUT BUTTER CUBE-CUPS

Homemade peanut butter cups are a good way to get a rep as someone who makes everything him- or herself, as they are not on most people's radar as something you can do at home. And yet they are oh so easy, especially as you can buy the chocolate in manageable amounts at the store. For this treat you don't need to do a **Janine Antoni** and chew it off a 600-pound block.

A really nice thing about the home-made peanut butter cup is that you can adapt it to your own preferences, be that for dark or milk chocolate, crunchy or smooth peanut butter. You can also fill your cups with other nut butters, like almond or cashew, or with chocolate icing, caramel, and even jam. All of these things are ready to use out of the jar. And guys, FYI: homemade chocolates will pretty much bring the house down on Valentine's Day (only we will know that it took you all of 10 minutes to do

Janine Antoni
Bahamian-born body and installation artist (b. 1964) who uses her body and its "tools" to paint and sculpt, mopping the floor with paint and her own hair, painting a canvas with tiny movements of her eyelashes, and sculpting heart-shaped boxes and lipsticks from massive chocolate and lard cubes by chewing off little bits with her own teeth in *Gnaw* (1992).

them). You don't need to be too much of a perfectionist with the look of these as you want them to have homemade charm, and you don't want to get overwhelmed in a **Bernhard and Anna Blume**-type "Kitchen Frenzy" and end up exhausted and irritable. That clearly would not be the point.

Get about four plain milk or dark chocolate bars of whatever kind you like. You should get 10 to 12 ounces of chocolate, so check the weight on the package and buy however many you need. The chocolate doesn't need to be fancy or expensive, just anything that tastes good to you.

Bernhard Blume and Anna Blume
German collaborative photographers (both b. 1937) who create sequences of images from Chaplinesque staged scenarios of humans struggling with obstacles, such as *Kitchen Frenzy*, a series of photographs of a woman (Anna Blume herself) having an all-out fit while trying to cook a pile of potatoes.

YOU'LL NEED
10–12 ounces ordinary chocolate bars
Plastic ice cube tray
Peanut butter or other filling

Break up and melt the chocolate bars in a small pot or metal bowl placed inside a bigger pot of boiling water (or an actual double boiler if you have one). This way the chocolate won't be on direct heat and will melt instead of burning. You can stir it a couple of times to speed the process. Melt until the chocolate is smooth. Take the chocolate off the heat and get to work right away before it hardens again.

Using a teaspoon, put a gob of chocolate in the bottom of one of the ice cube compartments and spread it up the sides to make the shell. Do the best you can to make sure that all sides and bottom are coated, without being super thick—the cube should be empty in the center. Do this for all the compartments. If your chocolate firms up too much to spread, you may have to put it back on the heat for a few moments to soften again. Put the ice cube tray in the freezer for a minute so the chocolate solidifies.

Take the tray out and put some filling into the center of each cube. This means spooning enough peanut butter (or other filling) into each compartment to fill it almost to the top. Put the tray back into the freezer for a minute so the peanut butter firms up. Meanwhile, remelt the rest of the chocolate.

When the chocolate's ready to go, bring out the ice cube tray and spoon the chocolate on the top of each cube, spreading to the edges so the peanut butter is covered. Obviously, the chocolate is not going to be perfectly neat, but this is the bottom. Let it be. As long as the peanut butter is sealed into the center of a chocolate cube, this is going to work. Put the tray back into the freezer for a few minutes.

Le Corbusier

Swiss architect and designer (1887–1965) known as "Corb" to architecture students. He was interested in Functionalism and collective housing, and envisioned a "vertical city" of skyscrapers with interior streets, though he didn't manage to build any of the latter.

When the chocolate has hardened, which is more or less immediately, you can take the tray out and pop the cubes out onto a plate. The tops will be all nice and smooth, so flip them over to face up—they look kind of like a modular housing project designed by **Corb,** don't they? You can refrigerate them until dessert time if it's hot out or keep them in the freezer if you like your treats icy cold. If they are meant as a gift, you can arrange them in a box on some tissue paper and tie a big, fat ribbon around the whole thing. Love and kisses will surely come your way.

This will produce about a dozen or so chocolates.

MOLE TRUFFLES

This recipe introduces a daring surprise to a traditional treat. Most people have heard of *mole*, that Mexican hot-and-spicy sauce that includes the surprising tastes of chocolate and cinnamon. Well, Mole Truffles are chocolate and cinnamon dessert treats with the surprising taste of Mexican hot-and-spiciness. It's a devilish twist, really.

Most truffle recipes use solid, semisweet, or unsweetened baking chocolate. This one I invented with powdered cocoa for the simple reason that my mom is always giving me cocoa powder as a gift. Since I (and probably some of you—could my mom possibly be the only one?) have cocoa powder around the house for making hot chocolate, etc., and would rather not make a trip to the store for baking chocolate, I developed the recipe accordingly.

YOU'LL NEED
8 tablespoons (1 stick) sweet butter
10 tablespoons unsweetened cocoa powder
Pinch or two of cayenne or chili pepper
10 tablespoons confectioners' sugar
5 tablespoons heavy cream
Powdered cinnamon

In a saucepan over low heat, melt the butter halfway. Turn off the heat and stir in the cocoa and cayenne while the butter continues to melt and cool at the same time. Add the sugar and whisk together.

Andres Serrano

American photographer (b. 1950) who explores religious symbolism and whose 1987 *Piss Christ* (a photo of a crucifix inside a container of urine) caused scandal and accusations of blasphemy. Jesse Helms said in the U.S. Senate in reference to the work, "He is not an artist, he is a jerk."

When the mixture becomes uniform, remove from the stove. Gradually whisk in the cream. Put this into the refrigerator until it becomes firm—probably overnight.

Put a few tablespoons of the cinnamon in a bowl. Make a small ball of the chocolate mixture with your hands or a melon baller, and drop in the cinnamon. Roll the ball around till it gets coated and then remove to a plate. Continue to make balls and then refrigerate them again until ready to serve. These will be surprising.

It's not as sacrilegious as **Serrano**'s *Piss Christ* or anything, but it will still raise some shocked eyebrows—though actually it tastes really good. Speaking of eyebrows, shocks, and Mexicans, you could try suggesting to people that Mole Truffles were **Frida Kahlo**'s favorite recipe, and that she made some for **Trotsky** the evening before he got the ice pick in the head (the more gullible among your friends might believe it).

Frida Kahlo   Mexican Surrealist painter (1907–1954) played by the inappropriately beautiful Salma Hayek in the movie *Frida*, and known for her many self-portraits and her signature flat, colorful canvases, replete with symbolism reflecting her Mexican heritage. Kahlo was married to Mexican muralist and heart-breaking philanderer Diego Rivera (see page 40), though she had affairs of her own, notably with Leon Trotsky.

Leon Trotsky   Russian revolutionary (1879–1940) who was booted out of Russia by the paranoid Stalin after Lenin's death and later assassinated in Mexico with an ice pick. Apparently he was the model for the ousted pig Snowball in George Orwell's allegorical novel of 1946, *Animal Farm*.

PART TWO

Home Decorating

Decorating your home in a unique way is crucial for a dynamic and original environment that inspires artistic possibility. Stainless steel everything gets a little bit soulless after a while. You can paint your apartment in a variety of bright and easy ways, and we all need some kind of furniture, although the bare mattress on the floor and the turned-over-crate bedside table have their own charms, for sure. You can always spin your decor as Japanese-inspired Minimalism and leave the place empty. At any rate, I think even Starving Artists agree that furniture at its best is useful, often comfortable, aesthetically appealing, and in an urban, rental culture is one of the most concrete methods we have of personalizing our transitional environments. But what is furniture really? Do you have to buy it? No! Can you make it yourself? Sure!

A Starving Artist might use industrial packaging as a coffee table or stackable plastic baker's trays as a flat file. An old bucket or a sink can be a planter. A colander or a circular air filter is a lamp shade, while a flattened and rusting soda can, or a child's dress, hung on a wall is an artifact. Any flat slab of found wood or stone can be a tabletop. Any small, heavy object can be a bookend or door stop. A hubcap or a saw blade can be made into a clock. A chipped ceramic pitcher can become a lamp. An item manufactured for one purpose can be put to use in a whole new way. The bottom line is, if you like it and you can drag it home, you can use it.

While a wood shop and a facility for power tools help with the more traditional furniture pieces, a Starving Artist works with what's available and this may include one's own abilities, relative time to spare, and technical know-how. The point is, anybody can make furniture, be it an **Eames** chair or a giant, cushy roll of bubble wrap—it's just a question of making it your own way. With pre-cut and threaded steel pipes you can make sturdy furniture of all shapes and sizes without any tools at all.

Charles and Ray Eames American designers (Charles 1907–1978 and Ray 1922–1988) who were husband and wife. They created furniture designs out of molded plywood, most famously the curved lounge chair that's usually referred to as the "Eames chair," produced by Herman Miller.

If the bigger pieces scare you, the chapter includes plenty of do-it-yourself "housewares." This is a catch-all name for the little stuff— basically anything in the home that's not structural enough to be referred to as furniture, but just facilitates the general business of living. Try a bright fluorescent detergent bottle wall sconce, coasters from your chewed bubble gum (very **Arte Povera**) or some customized bedding. This section contains some of the easiest and most rewarding projects as there aren't many structural requirements, and you can choose from a wide range of materials. Enjoy.

Arte Povera An art movement beginning in the late 1960s. The name was coined by Italian art critic Germano Celant, and translates as "poor art," which refers to the use of humble "everyday" materials and the all-inclusive experimental quality of the work. Participants include Jannis Kounellis (remembered best for his installation of twelve live horses in a Rome gallery, which is not so "poor" in a certain sense), Mario Merz, Alighiero Boetti, and Giovanni Anselmo.

Walls and Wall Treatments

OP ART DECORATING

Can't decide what color to paint your bathroom? Don't. Too intimidated to try sponging or faux finish? Rightly so. That stuff is fussy and time-consuming. Mesmerized by all the beautiful paint sample choices? Of course you are. Everyone knows paint chips are nicer than paint. Here's the solution for the best-ever, no-decision, funky, **Bridget Riley**-inspired decor, particularly good for hallways and bathrooms, where there's not much visual competition from furniture:

Bridget Riley American Op Art painter (b. 1931), influential in the 1960s and 1970s as a result of her abstract canvases, which play with geometric forms and the idea of "perception" as subject via optical illusion and lots of psychedelic striping.

Op Art An art movement of the 1960s. The name refers to "optical illusion," and the goal of the artists was to create an impression of movement through (usually abstract) mathematical control of color and form (think squares on top of more squares and wavy lines). Most memorable artists of the genre are painters Victor Vasarely and Bridget Riley. Considered part of the Op Art movement at least some of the time are Josef Albers, Richard Anuszkiewicz (pronounced a-noo-SKAY-vich), Kenneth Noland, and even M. C. Escher of the never-ending staircase and other famously clever drawings.

YOU'LL NEED

1 paint strip in the color range of your choice

5–6 quarts total chosen latex paint colors

1 quart white latex paint

Ordinary painting supplies (primer, brushes,
   rollers, tray, rags)

Roll of masking tape

Tape measure

Pencil

Vinyl stick-on letters (optional)

Take whatever strip of colors you find yourself hovering over most often. With most major paint brands (Dutch Boy, Glidden, Pratt & Lambert) you will be looking at between five and eight different shades. Now, instead of buying 2 gallons of any one color, run out to the hardware store and grab a quart of every color on the strip. Paint wide horizontal stripes of each shade, with a thin strip of white between them. When it dries, neatly frame your inspirational paint chip and hang it brazenly on the wall or door for a bit of the **Post-Modern** touch.

Post-Modern   Contemporary cultural theory that in reaction to Humanism (the mainstay of Western thought since the Enlightenment), uses "deconstruction" as its primary tool to break down assumptions and culture biases, and attempts to show that there are no universal truths but only "narratives" constructed by circumstance. Post-Modernism was made famous by such critics and philosophers as Mikhail Bakhtin, Ludwig Wittgenstein, Roland Barthes, and Jacques Lacan.

Deep Sea

High Tide

Shimmer Lake

Mountain Pool

Airy Breeze

Cloud Fluff

Keep any leftover paint for necessary touch-ups.

You won't need any more than the painting supplies you would use for one color (a white primer, brushes, rollers, trays, and rags). In addition, for this project, a tape measure will help you figure out your wall height (divide the height in inches by the number of colors to figure the thickness of the stripes) and some masking tape will make the lines and ensure a crisp edge if you like things super-neat.

If you want to get really "**contemporary art,**" you can get stick-on vinyl letters and spell out the name of each color (go for black or silver so "Shimmering Sea" and "Still Tidewater" will stand out beautifully). Stick the names on the wall at one end of each stripe just like in the paint sample.

Contemporary Art The latest in a series of terms originally used to describe work that was "current," but that ultimately came to define the era that coined them (i.e., Modern Art, which no longer means present-day art but rather art of the first half of the twentieth century). "Contemporary" generally refers to any art created post-1960 and seems to be shaping up to include work that uses either Post-Modern sensibilities or just lots of video and digital media. Nobody's quite sure yet.

REAL RAG ROLLING

A nicely textured wall treatment is a result of one thing—subtlety. The softly blurred paint application of a **Rothko** can encompass the meaning of life in a gentle wash. Doing this yourself is not hard if you don't give yourself the opportunity to mess it up—this means keeping your colors so similar that even an egregious mistake will hardly show.

To start, choose three shades of a color. Pale yellows are popular for this effect, but it is up to you, as long as the three are right next to each other on the paint chip, meaning they vary only slightly in intensity. You can do a combination of whites for a **Robert Ryman** effect, which looks awesome.

Robert Ryman

American Minimalist painter (b. 1930) who eventually worked entirely in white to avoid the "distraction" of color and to aid him in his ultimate goal of painting "to paint the paint."

YOU'LL NEED

3 paint colors of your choosing

Old cotton T-shirt or other rag

Roller and tray

Mark Rothko

Latvian-born American Color Field/Ab Ex painter (1903-1970). The painter of moody, soft-edged panels of layered and luminous rectangular color. Rothko's story perpetuates the image of the artist as tragically misunderstood and self-destructive, due in large part to the suicide that ended his life. His paintings are perceived as highly spiritual and profound, and he has been quoted as saying, in opposition to the modern notion that painting should be strictly about paint, "There is no such thing as good painting about nothing."

Roll your walls as usual with a single coat of the darkest shade (prime first if the pre-existing color will show through). Allow the paint to dry. Then, taking your rag, wrap it around a clean roller and tie it in place. Avoid loose ends, which will get loaded with paint and flap around annoyingly. Cut them off now before you begin. Make sure the roller is bound thoroughly and has a lumpy, irregular appearance, which should happen naturally if you tie the rag tightly.

Roll on a layer of the medium color with this rag roller. Because the roller isn't smooth, you will see that it doesn't cover completely, leaving a mottled appearance of dabs and blotches. Allow this color to dry. Create a new rag roll and paint on the lightest color. You should make sure that some of each color shows and you should find a softly variegated coloring that is not too speckly.

As you get more confident with this technique you can try varying the colors for more vivid effects, as in the work of **Joan Mitchell** or **Willem de Kooning,** two masters of messy brushwork, either of whom could probably paint a wall texture like nobody's business. If anybody ever asked them to.

Willem de Kooning Dutch-born American Ab Ex painter (1904–1997). His "Action" paintings tended to be semi-figurative, and though he is remembered as one of the creators of Abstract Expressionism, he is generally more expressionistic than abstract. De Kooning's works are masses of brightly colored and ferocious brushstrokes with an emphasis on process; famous is his *Woman* series of rough, piggy-faced women with big breasts. Robert Rauschenberg (see page 190) made art headlines with the piece *Erased de Kooning Drawing* (1953), which was, in fact, an erased de Kooning drawing, labeled and framed. The story goes that Robert got Willem's permission before wiping out his work.

Joan Mitchell American Ab Ex painter (1926–1992) who is not Joni Mitchell the musician (although that Mitchell is also a painter of sorts), but the creator of large abstract canvases of intensely vivid color and brushy markings.

AB EX FLOOR OR TABLETOP

This technique is perfect for a rough floor or table surface, or for anything that needs a touch of the dripped and spattered, **Jackson Pollock** wildness. Of course, J.P. is not the only painter to let the drips fly. **Sam Francis**'s influence might make for a fantastic look as well, and if you spill any large pools of paint, you can incorporate it as a **Helen Frankenthaler** motif. Choose your drip painter and go for it.

Ab Ex   Abstract Expressionist movement in postwar painting, which grew to huge prominence via the writing of critic Clement Greenberg and the artwork of Jackson Pollock, Willem de Kooning, Mark Rothko, Robert Motherwell, Helen Frankenthaler, and many others.

Jackson Pollock   American Ab Ex painter (1912–1956) and creator of "drip" paintings, carefully balanced by harmonic arrangements of poured colors weaving across the canvas. "Discovered" by Peggy Guggenheim and married to the painter Lee Krasner. His marriage and other details of his train wreck of a personal life were played out in the movie *Pollock* by actor-director Ed Harris, the Cliff's Notes being that he was a self-destructive, manic-depressive alcoholic who ultimately killed himself as well as a rarely remembered young woman in a drunk-driving accident on Long Island.

Sam Francis   American Ab Ex painter and printmaker (1923–1994) who created canvases of huge spatters and drips and was part of the Bay Area Abstract group.

Helen Frankenthaler   American Ab Ex/Color Field painter (b. 1928) who painted on unprimed canvas, giving her works a stained and pooled quality, different from the Ab Ex painters with whom she's generally associated.

YOU'LL NEED

Enamel paint for base coat
Enamel paint for spatter coat
2 stirring sticks or 1 stick and 1 brush
Newspaper or plastic drop cloths
Masking tape

First, prepare your work area: this means masking, with newspaper or plastic, anything that would be adversely affected by unanticipated paint spatters. For a floor this would require taping newspaper around the baseboards, extending 2 to 3 feet up the wall and lightly secured at the top to keep in place. For a tabletop project, give yourself lots of space and lay newspapers on the floor in the surrounding areas, as well as taping paper to cover the sides of your table if the top is not detachable—you don't want paint drips running down the sides.

Then, using the enamel paint, cover your surface with a base color—white is fine for this project as paint spatter can get busy—and allow it to dry according to the directions on your can. You can go for a strictly black-and-

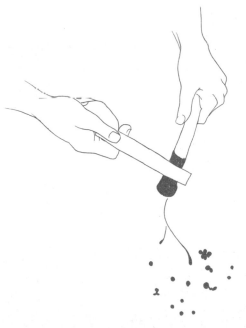

white image on this project, which is what I did on my bathroom floor, or mix up two or three colors for a brighter, busier look. Dip a brush or stirring stick into the paint can. Take another stick and bang the two against each other over your surface. Droplets will disperse. You can also flick the paint off the stick with a quick back-and-forth motion of the wrist, which will cause more long strands and swirls of the paint to form. Both are nice.

If you are covering a floor, you'll need to back your way across the room toward the door, flicking paint as you go and stepping out the doorway at the end to avoid walking on and tracking wet paint.

This can be a surprisingly beautiful effect, and if you spatter the surface fairly uniformly and avoid getting paint on other things, it won't look messy, but rather as harmonious as a masterpiece should.

SCRIBBLE WALL

This is a good technique for a foyer wall where you want some introductory Starving Artist funk, but you don't have anything special to hang. Drawing directly on the wall is so daringly **Sol Le Witt,** allowing you to become part of the very architecture of your home.

YOU'LL NEED
White latex primer
Masking tape
Pencil

Sol Le Witt
American conceptual artist (b. 1928) known for his early focus on ranking process over product, with the creation of modular cube structures to be dismantled after a show and subsequently rearranged, as well as *Wall Drawings,* works to be created directly on the gallery's interior surfaces.

Pick a wall for the project and paint it a color you like, allowing the paint to dry fully before proceeding further. Measure out a neat rectangle of masking tape in the wall's center (the dimensions could be anything; you might try 3 × 4 feet), then roll on a double coat of white latex primer within the masking tape (doesn't matter if the paint gets onto it, but don't let it go outside the tape). The project works best if the scribbles are bordered by an extremely clean-edged rectangle, so take care that your masking tape is laid on straight and smooth before beginning with the white primer.

When you are finished painting, you will have a neat, white rectangle on your wall. Leaving the tape for now, allow the paint to dry. Using an ordinary pencil, start filling the area with some **Cy Twombly** scribbles, right up to the tape. These would probably consist of loose elliptical lines, as if you were making a sloppy series of cursive e's. You can also just place a stack of pencils on a small table and sanction the scribbling of notes and messages as long as they fit in the white space. If your rectangle is located near a hall phone or message table, it will look particularly apropos as an ode to the phone message or absent-minded doodle. **Sigmar Polke** made a meandering piece called *Telephone Drawing* that you might look at for inspiration.

Remove the tape border when finished.

Cy Twombly American Gestural Expressionist painter and sculptor (b. 1928) who is known for his unmistakable paintings of scribbles, the later of which include some recognizable text and numbers.

Sigmar Polke German Pop Art painter (b. 1941) who, along with fellow Germans Gerhard Richter and Konrad Lueg Fischer, founded what they called Capitalist Realism, a variant of Pop Art that humorously critiques consumerism and mass production. Polke often used patterned canvases as background for his cartoony, layered imagery, and in later years he began experimenting with unfamiliar pigments and other potentially unstable materials.

Visitors will be intrigued by your original masterpiece, and you can always paint over it if you move out or lose interest. Best of all, you've got a work of art hanging, but no holes in the wall!

Note: An alternative method for this project is to paint an entire wall white and allow freeform scribbles and the leaving of messages by all members of the household; you might get some **Basquiat**-type drawings in the mix—see what happens. When the scribble urge has gotten out of everyone's system, mask a tape rectangle around your favorite section of wall and prime and paint the wall all around this rectangle a different color, leaving only this one section covered with scribbling.

Jean-Michel Basquiat   American Neo-Expressionist painter (1960–1988). A native New Yorker of Puerto Rican/Haitian descent, Basquiat began his career as a street graffiti artist and shot to fame quickly, soon collaborating on pieces with Andy Warhol and selling his own paintings like hotcakes. The film *Basquiat*, directed by fellow art star Julian Schnabel, chronicles his brief, brilliant career, abruptly cut short by the overdose that ended his life. Check out almost any major museum for examples of his humorously drawn but elegant and poignant paintings.

RAMSHACKLE ROOM DIVIDER

If you ever find yourself wanting to separate a room, but are afraid your landlord might freak out, or you can't afford the materials to make real walls, painter Jessica Dickinson's clever room-within-a-room shed is a creative solution. This provides a **Margaret Kilgallen** feeling of authentic down-and-out charm right in your own bedroom. You can create a walk-in closet or a private workroom this way, and add luxury and good feng shui to a one-room studio or an awkwardly shaped apartment. Just be sure to check out local fire codes.

Margaret Kilgallen American installation artist and muralist (1967–2001) with an interest in Americana and lettering. Old signage often appears in her works and contributes to the evocation of a cartoonish skid row atmosphere.

My friend Jessica made this shack in her loft as a way to create a bedroom and studio space for herself in the midst of a home shared with three roommates. To complete the project, she spent some time collecting a small heap of "supplies" (aka debris) from the industrial fringes of the neighborhood—things like the sides of old wooden crates, old windows, planks, and bits of plywood. Jessica's tiny shack is just large enough to fit the bed and dresser, but leaves the rest of her room free for a work and painting space.

YOU'LL NEED

Enough 2×4s to frame your shack walls, pre-cut to size

Found pieces of old wood for the walls

Plenty of screws and a power screwdriver

Brackets and hinges (optional)

Jigsaw to cut the pieces (or fit them like puzzle pieces, allowing overlap when necessary to avoid cutting)

Latex paint to cover the finished wall (optional)

If you've never built a wall before and are nervous or find the instructions hard to visualize, check out *The Reader's Digest New Complete Do-It-Yourself Manual*, which will explain in greater detail how it's done and take you through it step by step. My friend Tobias swears by this book, and he is super handy and knows how to build all kinds of stuff anyway, so it must be good. Making a wall is not really too hard, although working with a friend will make things a lot easier as the pieces can feel big and unwieldy. Although, part of the point of this wall design is that it doesn't include huge sheets of Sheetrock for facing the walls, and as a result is a rare wall concept that is manageable to build as a solo project.

Using 2×4s, build a frame for the walls. This means screwing horizontal 2×4s to both the floor and the ceiling as supports, and screwing vertical 2×4s to the supports at the ends and at 16-inch intervals. If your room will be freestanding, you can build your frames flat on the floor and then stand them up, bracing the sides to each other at the corners with angled pieces across the top. Otherwise, you can screw the frame into the walls or floor for sturdiness. Then screw the found pieces of wood to the frame, from stud to stud. They can overlap each other if you don't have a jigsaw to cut them to fit. You don't have to cover both sides of your frame, either, unless you want to go super pro and put insulation in the middle.

For a door, use a combination of large pieces with metal brackets holding them together on both sides until you have a structure big enough to fill the door opening. Attach this door to the frame with hinges. Jessica has a door that hinges in several sections, like a barn door. You can also paint the whole wooden structure a single color for a **Louise Nevelson**-type effect. Either way, it will look really good and afford you some cheaply made privacy at the same time.

> ## Louise Nevelson
>
> Ukrainian-born American assemblage artist (1900–1988) whose cobbled, wooden, giant wallpieces are painted a uniform black. She is arguably the first American woman sculptor recognized as important.

MAGNET WALL

Massive shapes of metal give off that comfortable feeling of being nicely ensconced in the Modernist tradition. Also comfy is the awareness that you are playing on the impressive team of such heavy hitters as **Gropius** and the entire gamut of Minimalist sculptors.

Photographer and documentary filmmaker Kirsten Johnson contributed this idea for a slick home-

> ## Walter Gropius
>
> German Modernist architect (1883–1969) and founder of the Bauhaus (no, not the 1980s New Wave band, the German art school that they swiped their name from) who emigrated to America and became a professor at Harvard. Gropius and the Bauhaus architects are one of the prime examples of European influence on the American landscape about which Tom Wolfe had such a hissy fit, decrying it with fervor in his book *From Bauhaus to Our House*.

office over-the-desk magnet bulletin board. It's a great way to stay organized without letting that same organization make you feel like you've become fussy and constricted.

Bring a magnet along (or ask questions) when you go shopping for your metal sheet—some types of stainless steel are nonmagnetic.

YOU'LL NEED

Standard 25-gauge uncut sheet of magnetic steel to measure 8×4-feet (or cut as appropriate if this won't fit your space)

Sheet metal screws and power screwdriver

Magnets and stuff to hang

Screw the metal sheet flat onto the wall with the sheet metal screws at the corners and every 2 feet or so along the edge to prevent buckling. Feel free to hang stainless steel baskets or any racks normally meant for the kitchen or bathroom onto this surface as well. Working with that large piece of metal on your own could make you feel like you've taken on the monumental task of building a **Richard Serra,** although if you get someone to help you hold the metal sheet while you attach it, it won't be hard to manage and nowhere near as over-

Richard Serra American Minimalist sculptor (b. 1939) known best for his macho manipulations of monumentally sized sheets of steel, as in *Torqued Ellipses* (1996–99), which curve in and away while they tower high overhead. He was also at the center of a big 1980s flap about the role of public art when office workers complained that *Tilted Arc* (1981), the sculpture he'd made for New York's Federal Plaza, wasn't terribly conducive to relaxing and eating lunch. The sculpture was eventually removed.

whelming as his towering shapes. Imagine if you were heading the crew responsible for the installation of one of his giants! Your sheet is only about ¹⁄₁₀₀th of the size, after all.

Finally, you'll need some magnets for sticking things up onto your new wall. You can make nice ones by gluing Hot Glue Jewels (see page 191) or old, cool buttons to plain round magnets sized to fit beneath them. Or, many film developers will print any photo onto a magnet for a reasonable price. You can do a **Joseph Kosuth**-type existential series by taking photos of all your office supplies like staplers, pens, Scotch tape, lamps, and desk chairs and turning those into magnets to stick up above the originals. Or you might even try a series of blown-up photo-magnets of metal screws, like the ones you used to screw up your magnet wall—very self-referential and arty.

> **Joseph Kosuth**   American conceptual artist (b. 1945), renowned for his *One and Three Chairs* (1965), a reflection on aspects of perception that included an actual chair, a photo of the same chair, and a mounted dictionary definition of a chair. In later works Kosuth dispensed entirely with the real objects and the photos and presented nothing but the lone definitions of things printed onto large text cards.

CHAPTER SIX

Furniture

POP ART TOMATO TABLE

Making furniture is not all about mastering the use of the table saw or the router. It's not just about wood grain or sandpaper. There was a time when that was so, but in the post–space age, it's not only possible but downright stylish to infuse your furniture collection with the synthetic modishness of a mid-career **Stanley Kubrick** film. Remember, the 1960s were not all about men with long hair and women with bare breasts. They were also the decade of Nancy Sinatra in knee-high walkin' boots, Pop as art, and a resulting new sophistication about what it means to be original. As far as furniture goes, I have one word for you: *plastics.*

Plexiglas is a brand name for solid acrylic, or what we normally think of

Pop Art An artistic movement emerging first in England in the 1950s with artists David Hockney and Richard Hamilton, and subsequently flourishing in New York City of the 1960s and early 70s. Pop Art's "cool" sensibility was considered a reaction to the high-minded seriousness of Abstract Expressionism and was meant to play with the distinction between "high" and "low" art and explore issues of mass media and popular culture. Paintings and sculpture represented everyday objects and images from advertising and commercial art. Some of the most famous Pop artists include Roy Lichtenstein, Jasper Johns, Sigmar Polke, Robert Rauschenberg, Claes Oldenburg, James Rosenquist, Jim Dine, Edward Ruscha (pronounced *roo-SHAY*), and Keith Haring.

as hard plastic. Obviously you don't need to use any particular brand, just the least expensive one you can find. Look in the yellow pages under "Plastics—Suppliers" or "Signs" and find someone who can cut sheets to size for you. In addition, the size of your project can be adapted to what sort of pieces you find pre-cut. This can save you a lot of money, as getting plastic to spec can often entail buying an entire large sheet. Be flexible. I created this table design by browsing for remnant scraps at an industrial plastics store near me.

Stanley Kubrick   American filmmaker (1928–1999) whose famed oeuvre includes something from almost every film genre imaginable, as well as the futuristically designed *2001: A Space Odyssey* and *A Clockwork Orange*. Kubrick is beloved by film buffs, and I've been pointing out for years that ultimate film-geek-turned-director Quentin Tarantino remade Kubrick's heist movie, *The Killing*, as his own heist movie, *Reservoir Dogs*. I've never heard it acknowledged officially, but I'm vindicated now, as the authors of *The Hipster Handbook* apparently noticed the same thing.

YOU'LL NEED

1 1/4-inch-thick square of red acrylic, 16 inches on each side, for top

1 1/8-inch-thick square of clear acrylic, 8 inches on each side, for base

1 24-inch-long clear acrylic tube, 3 inches in diameter

10 fake plastic tomatoes or other fruit to fit in tube

clear-drying epoxy

Q-tip

Making the table is incredibly easy once you have gathered your materials. Wipe clean the inside of your clear tube and then glue it, centered, onto the square base. You'll find the center by measuring the base diagonally from corner to corner and marking the midpoint of the line. Then measure perpendicular to this line, bisecting the opposite corners, and find the midpoint again. Make a tiny mark with a grease pencil or bit of soap—this is your center. Position your acrylic tube so it is exactly surrounding this center point. Take a Q-tip saturated with the glue and press into the seam where the tube meets the flat base, inching around the tube and re-saturating the Q-tip with glue when needed. Allow this to dry undisturbed for at least 10 minutes (or according to the glue's directions).

Stack the 10 tomatoes in the tube or as needed to fill up. This part of the table will resemble a piece by **Arman,** with its items all crammed in. You can also fill the tube with other objects, but the tomatoes are particularly nice because if you get the correct size tubing they will stack very neatly one on top of the other.

> **Arman**   French-born American assemblage artist (b. 1928). Arman created many works of found materials, which presage installation art. He constructed "accumulations," his name for groups of similar objects crammed willy-nilly into containers.

Place the tabletop facedown on your work surface, and find the center again. Place the tube and base upside down onto the center mark. Make sure the sides of the base are squared with the sides of the top. Glue the cylinder to the top and allow it to dry.

Flip over the table onto its base and admire it. Yup, that's good.

HANGING "MURPHY" SHELF

While I personally think that the whole stainless-steel-at-every-turn look is getting overplayed, there's an undeniable slickness to metal furniture that can be clean and appealing. Particularly in the kitchen, stainless gives off that industrial "pro" vibe and serves to make you feel like you've got your own li'l restaurant and that Mario might be stopping by later. Anything that makes cooking at home more pleasant is a good thing when it comes to saving bucks.

This is a swank-looking shelving idea that mimics the industrial baker's racks you find in professional kitchens and can be tucked up against the wall if you need to get it out of the way. This project is, of course, for the penniless (i.e., you and me) rather than the penny-laden, who without thought pay major bucks for industrially styled kitchen accessories. This shelf is stylish in the kitchen if you need extra shelf space, but can work in any room. It also makes an end table or bedside table, or a **Donald Judd**-style wall sculpture—especially if you do multiples.

Donald Judd
American Minimalist sculptor (1928–1994). His "stacks," vertical installations of identical manufactured metal or plastic slabs distributed mathematically, are his most recognizable pieces.

YOU'LL NEED

An old oven rack (see suggestions for finding and cleaning below)

Plumber's pipe hanger

Drywall screws

2 yards of light-gauge aircraft cable

2 eyehooks

The surface of the shelf is an old oven rack. You can find these by going out on the appropriate garbage night in your neighborhood and opening some of the old stoves you see sitting on the curb. Most municipalities have one night a week designated for large or metal refuse, and if you call the local sanitation department, they can let you know when the stoves are

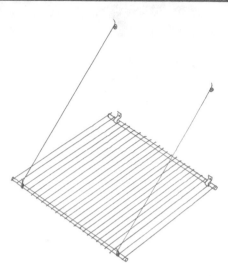

tossed out. Take along a rubber glove if you're easily made queasy, and put the rack in a plastic garbage bag to bring it home (although if you are easily made queasy you probably dropped this book back when I mentioned *Piss Christ* in the Mole Truffle recipe and are no longer reading at this juncture).

If the rack needs cleaning, just sprinkle it liberally with baking soda and spray with water and leave it overnight in its bag. Rinse in the morning and repeat if necessary.

To hang the shelf with style you'll need some metal gadgetry—all available at a decent hardware store. Attach the back edge of the shelf to the wall with two or three short hinges made of plumber's pipe hanger. To screw the rack into the wall, you'll need to locate a stud in the wall and screw into that, or use a "butterfly" to keep your screw secure in the wall. Make sure you hang the shelf level unless "crooked" is the specific look you're going for. To the front edge of the rack, attach two pieces of aircraft cable and then loop them into sturdy eyehooks fastened to the wall. Place the eyehooks level with each other, creating an isosceles triangle between the wall and the oven rack and thus creating the "Murphy" effect—remember those fold-down beds? For those of you who can't remember geometry well enough to know what I mean by the word *isosceles,* fold up the shelf against the wall and mark where the top edge reaches. This is where you attach the ends of the cables.

The nicest part of this shelf is that you can hang baskets onto it from underneath, as well as stacking things on the top. It provides a very practical amount of space and the look is oh so modern and **minimalist**.

> **Minimalism** Considered by some artists (most vocally Judd and Flavin) to be an insult (because of the obvious connotation of simplistic-ness), Minimalism refers to art of the late 1960s /70s (including music, design, etc.), which is characterized by a spare and unfussy quality.

FAKE ANTIQUING

Who doesn't fantasize about the thrill of finding a genuine antique stuck out with the trash? Is it possible that somewhere out there are people who don't even cast a glance at the discarded chairs on the curb awaiting pickup? Of course, but those people couldn't possibly be Starving Artists. The problem with the "waiting" plan is that you could wait forever for a real antique to turn up. So, for the impatient or the take-charge-of-your-own-destiny types, here's a way to up your odds by turning almost any piece of furniture into a "piece." There's also a time-honored tradition of forgery in the arts, addressed in particularly fascinating style in film demigod

Orson Welles's documentary of sorts, *F for Fake*.

This technique can dress up crappy wood street furniture (i.e., the kind that someone else is throwing away, not the kind for sitting out on the sidewalk in the evening) like nobody's business. Or, you can buy inexpensive unfinished wood furniture and instantly give it an old and unique feel. The Starving Artist's Way is to have special, one-of-a-kind furniture, not the stuff that prompts people who come over for dinner to say, "Oh, I have that same table from Ikea."

YOU'LL NEED

Your piece of furniture
A few sheets of medium-grit and
    fine-grit sandpaper
A white candle
3 different colors of latex paint
    (you might try red, white,
    and blue)

Orson Welles American filmmaker (1915–1985) who directed *Citizen Kane*, considered by many to be the greatest movie of all time. Welles also made *Touch of Evil*, which has an opening sequence choreographed across four blocks and made from one single shot of unedited film. His early fame came from *War of the Worlds* (1939), a radio play that caused a panicky and apparently gullible public to think planet Earth was actually being invaded by creatures from outer space. *F for Fake*, Welles's examination of forgery and deception in art, leaves you wondering why you ever bother to believe anything.

Lightly sand the surface of your piece, and paint a coat of latex paint onto all visible areas. Allow to dry. Take the candle and rub it thickly and roughly on to the edges and corners of the furniture and in patches on any large surface areas. You won't really see the wax, but that's the idea. Take a second paint color and paint roughly over the piece again, primarily over the waxy areas, but covering an even larger area and some new spots, too. You don't need to fully cover the piece of furniture with this coat. Allow the paint to dry.

Take some fine-grit sandpaper and sand it lightly over the piece, focusing on the areas where you've applied the wax. Because the paint will not adhere securely over the wax, you'll find that rubbing the waxed areas causes paint to come away easily with a patchy effect. Brush off the sanding residue and rub wax again onto the newly painted areas.

Choose the final coat of paint. This will be the main color of the piece and can be light or dark. Cover the piece completely with the third paint color and allow it to dry. Sand the piece again in the same manner, removing sections of the top coat and revealing layers of the two colors underneath. You'll have a layered-paint effect

> **Antoni Tàpies**
> Spanish Ab Ex painter (b. 1923) known for textured paintings, incorporating clay and marble dust that have been sanded and scraped, collaged, and graffitied.

worthy of **Tàpies** himself. Ta da: instant, weather-worn antique. People will think it's a special find. Tell the suckers how to do it, if you want.

MILK CARTON LAMINATE FURNITURE

This is the best idea ever for leftover cartons from cereal or milk or anything else, created by architect/designer Jesse Levin. From the cartons you can make laminate sheets, which you can then use the same way as you use plywood. These sheets can be cut with wood tools, routed, drilled—you name it—and you can make them into anything you want. Jesse has made furniture, crates, and all kinds of other pieces from this material. The milk cartons are especially nice to use, as the waxy coating means you don't need any kind of protective varnish for the surface, and whatever project you make will have the packaging imagery on the surface.

YOU'LL NEED

A heap of cartons

Wood glue

2 flat boards big enough to cover the finished piece (that you are OK about drilling holes into)

Homemade comb (see below)

2 1×4-inch sticks of wood that can span the length of your piece

2 clamps

You'll need to disassemble all your cartons so that you have flat pieces of cardboard. You'll be laying them out in layers to reach your desired thickness. Drill holes into your wood boards every 4 inches or so to let air through.

Saving your nicest cartons for the top layer, lay out your first layer of carton pieces on one board and have the next layer handy. Coat the tops of the cartons lightly with wood glue thinned 7:1 with water and applied with a comb cut from thin wood or stiff cardboard. The mixture should be quite thinly applied so the glue appears clear, not yellow, on the surface of the cardboard. Make sure you cover the surface completely. Coat the pieces for the second layer of cardboard and then lay them, glue to glue, onto the first. Continue in this way until you have reached the desired thickness for your board. All this glue and cardboard is going to seem like a **Tom Sachs** copycat project, but unlike one of his pieces, the glue dribbles won't be a visible aspect of the finished work.

> **Tom Sachs** American contemporary artist (b. 1966) whose signature format is collaged sculptures of glued bits of packaging that become recognizable objects, often guns. Sachs was roundly criticized for his *Prada Death Camp* (1999), a model concentration camp built from a designer hat box.

Place the second wooden board on top of your layers and clamp the two boards together with the 1×4-inch sticks of wood under the clamps and spanning their width (this evens the distribution of the clamping weight). Allow at least 24 hours for your laminate to dry.

When you remove the laminate from its clamps, you will have a solid board and can do anything you want to it: cut it and screw it together and build shelves or other furniture that are uniquely surfaced in red-and-white milk-carton text. Combine this with the pipe and flange building technique (see page 98) for a truly unique piece of furniture.

DIORAMA DOOR TABLE

A rchitectural salvage and other recyclables fuel many an interior decorator, and have come in handy for artists too, notably **Duchamp** with his "ready-mades"— although the late **Stephen Jay Gould**'s Art Science Research Laboratory has in recent years raised the interesting question of whether Duchamp's supposed relics were not actually cleverly configured fakes, slyly altered to test visual perception, rather than the ordinary detritus of twentieth-century life. I dunno.

I do know this, though: an old door is large and sturdy enough to make a great tabletop. It can be an oversize coffee table, or a way to seat several at dinner. Its base can be a support of stacked cinder blocks that have been "borrowed" from a demolished building, or a pipe and flange construction (see the following section). The best doors for this purpose are those with inset panels in the center, perfect for creating diorama-like 3-D collages, as suggested by Katy Chevigny, documentary filmmaker.

> **Marcel Duchamp**
> French Dadaist sculptor/painter (1887–1968), the title of whose *Nude Descending a Staircase* (1913) has become a sort of cliché of modern art. His *Fountain* (1917), a urinal signed "R. Mutt," is also a modern classic. Duchamp is also the man who put a mustache on the Mona Lisa. Toward the end of his life, he claimed to lose interest in art and became a chess player. Could there be an important lesson in that . . . ?

> **Stephen Jay Gould** American evolutionary biologist and professor (1941–2002) who wrote numerous books about science, notable for their popular accessibility. Gould asserted that our era is not dominated by us humans, but is more properly thought of as the "age of bacteria."

YOU'LL NEED

A door

A sheet of clear acrylic plastic (Plexiglas) cut to the size of your door and at least 1/4-inch thick for sturdiness

Screws (optional)

Potting soil, moss, or 2 distinct colors of pebbles or gravel from a garden center (white and black are stylish); you can also use buttons or beads if you have access to them cheaply, or any other filler you like.

Take the hardware (knob and hinges) off the door. Sand your door to remove any loose or flaky paint. I think an aged and worn "artifact" quality is perfect for the look of this project, so I wouldn't cover the door with a fresh coat of paint unless it's in really sorry shape.

The plastic will lie on top of the door, becoming the ultimate table-top surface. The gap in between is a perfect place to create some kind of "subterranean" centerpiece. You can attach the Plexiglas top permanently with drilled holes at each corner and screws. Or you can leave it loose and impermanent so you can change the interior contents for every dinner party you host. You can fill the gap with fresh moss or potting soil for a **Walter de Maria** *Earth Room*-like creation that brings a bit of nature right up to the table. Or do a Robert Smithson-inspired "spiral jetty" formation; for that you'll need the pebbles.

Walter de Maria

American environmental artist (b. 1935), whose *Earth Room* (1977) was a fixture of New York's SoHo for years. He was also an early drummer for the famed N.Y.C. rock band the Velvet Underground.

You can also do this with sand if you can't find pebbles small enough to fit under your plastic slab—remember that the plastic must lie smoothly on the outer edges of the door, so the table's contents must be shallow enough to fit in the recessed portions. Arrange the white stones in a spiral formation in the panel mimicking **Smithson**'s massive formation in the Great Salt Lake. Fill in around the spiral with the black stones. Lay the plastic on top. Set the table. Cook something. Have dinner. Enjoy the compliments from your guests, pour an extra glass of wine, etc.

Robert Smithson   American environmental artist (1938–1973). The "rock star" of twentieth-century artists, complete with a brief, spectacular career of grand-scale works and an early death in a plane crash while surveying a site for a proposed project. Smithson is best known for *Spiral Jetty* (1972), a massive swirl of rock in the Great Salt Lake of Utah, which has since been subsumed by the lake itself. His essay "A Tour of the Monuments of Passaic, New Jersey" (1967) reads like a witty introduction to the ideas of Post-Modernism in art.

Pipe and Flange Furniture

Making furniture out of threaded black steel pipe is all the rage among my artist friends, though the first person I saw do this was painter Chris Hopewell. A plumbing supply store will cut all the pipe pieces to size for you, and you can create really impressive sturdy and modern pieces with this method without much in the way of tools. Think of the whole idea as a giant Erector set, which can be built up in any number of ways. The surface can be wood, salvaged slabs of granite or marble, plastic, or sheet metal. Einstein claimed that if he could do it all over, he would have been a plumber, so there's got to be something to it.

THE VARIOUS PIPE PIECES YOU'LL NEED

Flange—This piece goes on the base end of an upright pipe to stand the piece on the floor. It has holes for attaching to a surface with screws.

Threaded Pipe—These are the legs and cross pieces. They are just metal pipes, but the thread-ing is what allows you to attach them to the flanges and other parts. They come in various di-ameters, which will make your piece sturdier or lighter, depending on what you choose; ½-inch or ¾-inch is sturdy enough for this purpose.

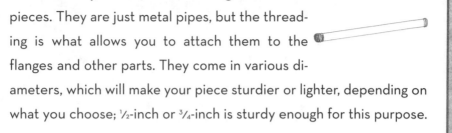

Elbow—Use these if you want to create a right angle of pipe. You could design your piece using entirely elbows and no flanges, if you prefer that look.

Tee—These go onto the pipe in order to attach a cross-brace to an upright. Large pieces will re-quire bracing in this way for sturdiness.

Giovanni Anselmo Italian Arte Povera sculptor (b. 1934) whose interest lies in studying the forces of na-ture and how they act on such ordinary materials as stone, water, plastic, and vegetables. The 1968 sculpture *Untitled* was constructed from a gran-ite block held in place by a head of lettuce.

You can design your own furniture easily by adapting the lengths of pipe to the piece you need or the tabletop you've found some-where. Some specific designs follow:

For example, lean a steel pipe against a wall and wait a millennium for its inevitable decay. Oh wait, that's not pipe-and-flange furniture, that's an art piece. And it was already done in 1969 by **Giovanni Anselmo.** You can do a re-make of that, if you like, or try one of the fol-lowing more traditional ideas.

WALL MOUNT SHELF

ctor Jason McKay designed this simple, no-sawing-necessary, wall-mounted pipe-and-flange shelf, which is made out of entire uncut boards straight from the lumberyard.

YOU'LL NEED

2 boards, 8 feet long by 12 inches wide
9 lengths of pipe, each 14 inches long and threaded
6 flanges
6 elbows
Drywall screws
Butterfly bolts

The boards are all you need for the surface. You can coat these with varnish if you wish, but allow them to dry before installing them.

You'll need 3 pipe brackets for this shelf. Each bracket is made out of two flanges, two elbows, and three lengths of pipe. The pipe threading allows you to insert the pipe into the flange opening and actually screw them together to tighten. Tighten the connection firmly so the pipe doesn't wobble. The same technique is used to fasten a pipe to an elbow. Once you thread the pieces together, you'll need to screw the brackets to the wall at 5½-foot distances, using butterfly bolts for support.

One shelf spans the lower pipe rungs, one lies on top. This is a beautiful, simple way to display a collection of turn-of-the-century miniature hand-carved ivory tortoises, or just to keep glasses in a kitchen.

BOOKSHELF

 simple bookshelf can be made to order with this pipe-and-flange technique, and every Starving Artist needs some books in his or her life, or at least a place to put this one. Adapt the lengths of the shelves to suit your space and circumstances. If you don't like books, you can slap a row of mini TVs into the middle of your shelf for a rip-off of a **Nam June Paik** installation piece. Maybe you can call it "entertainment center." The more TVs the better, really, if you're going the **Installation Art** route, and you can even skip the pipes entirely and build the whole thing out of a stack of old monitors.

Nam June Paik South Korean Fluxus video/installation artist (b. 1932), one of the founders of the Fluxus movement and known for such stunts as crafting a "TV Bra" to be worn during a performance by cellist Charlotte Moorman, as well as cutting off spectator-composer John Cage's necktie during a 1959 concert. Paik was transitioning then from experimental composer to full-fledged Fluxus artist, and mentor Cage (see page 149) was supposedly a good sport about the incident, allowing NJP to get away with this particular experiment in pushing the boundaries of acceptable performance.

Installation Art Art created to occupy a particular space ("site-specific"), using that space as a canvas to be filled with objects, redefined, painted, and so on.

YOU'LL NEED

4 legs of 18-inch-long pipe, threaded

2 threaded pipes, 12 inches, for each shelf you add

4 18-inch-long pieces of threaded pipe for each additional shelf

4 6-inch lengths of threaded pipe as connectors

4 6-inch lengths of threaded pipe for attaching top tee to elbow

2 threaded pipes, 4 feet long, for tops

2 threaded pipes, 12 inches long, for tops

4 flanges for the base

4 tees for every shelf you want to add

4 elbows for the top

4 tees for top

Desired number of 12-inch-wide planks, cut to 4-foot lengths to lie across the pipes, for the shelves

Thread a flange onto the base of each leg. Top each leg with a tee and then add the next piece of upright pipe. Finish the top with a tee, the short 6-inch pipe, and then an elbow. Attach the 12-inch cross pieces to each tee, making the shelf supports. At the top, attach the 4-foot lengths to the elbows to brace the shelf. Flanges can be screwed to the floor (when possible) for extra sturdiness.

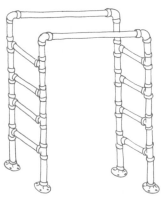

TOWEL RACK

A towel rack is the simplest of the pipe-and-flange constructions. You can make it from the thinnest pipe available, as you won't need much support.

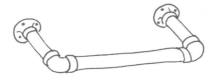

YOU'LL NEED

2 threaded pipes, 6 inches long

1 threaded pipe, 18 inches long

2 flanges

2 elbows

Thread all the pieces into each other. Screw the flanges into the wall at the appropriate height. Hang your fluffy towel on the rack and go make a humongous splash, like in a **Hockney** painting.

David Hockney English Pop Art painter and photo collagist (b. 1937) considered one of the creators of the Pop Art movement in 1950s England. Best known for *A Bigger Splash* (1967) and numerous other paintings of Los Angeles swimming pools, as well as his series of snapshot layouts of multiperspective approaches to a single moment or event. His *The Scrabble Game* (1983), for example, shows each player, each's stash of letters, the game board, and the progressing game, splayed out like a deck of cards on a flat surface.

TABLES

A table base can be made out of pipe and adapted to any tabletop or found piece of slate or other stone. This design can be put together several different ways, some of which lead to almost a **Noguchi** formation, an angle particularly enhanced if you use a see-through material for your tabletop. Keep in mind that your tabletop will rest on a pipe-and-flange base, so make sure the length and width of your pipes will support your surface comfortably.

Isamu Noguchi American sculptor, designer, and public artist (1904–1988). Influenced by his Japanese heritage in his public art and design work, Noguchi is currently most popularly appreciated for his design of a Herman Miller coffee table that features a glass top and unique sculptural base and the Akari standing lamp with a tall paper shade. Both of these designs have become known to the masses through the proliferation of the relatively inexpensive knock-offs that they spawned.

YOU'LL NEED

4 pieces of threaded pipe cut to 10-inch lengths and 4 pieces cut to 20-inch lengths

4 threaded pipes of the appropriate "width" for your table

2 threaded pipes of the appropriate "length" for your table

8 elbows

4 tees

Put together the base of your table by attaching elbows to a "width" pipe. Then put a 20-inch pipe into each elbow. Top with a tee and then add the next width pipe to it and then the 10-inch upright pipes to each side. Top each upright with another elbow. Create a matching piece and connect the two pieces together with the "length" pipes at the elbows. This creates a sturdy table base. Lay your surface onto this structure.

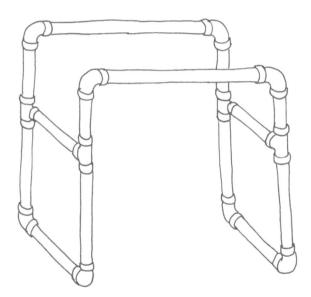

You can also make a table base that will screw into the underside of your tabletop if it's made of wood. Just make sure to put flanges on the tops of your table legs and use screws that are short enough so as not to go through the table surface. Use tees to brace the legs.

Housewares

"MY CHILD COULD PAINT THAT" ART

One of the keys to being a Starving Artist is being willing to play around, make a big mess, and take risks, always knowing that a "failed" project can turn into your biggest accomplishment. Messes may spark a random new idea, they may turn into a happily accidental masterpiece, or an attempted "fix" to a disaster may be the beginning of a whole new artistic technique.

Throughout the history of modern art there have been artists and artistic styles attempting to approximate the naiveté of children's art (**Jean Dubuffet** and Art Brut, et al.). At the same time, throughout the history of modern art there have been irritable and irritating members of the public who, on seeing canvases covered in drips and sloppy splashes, have complained, "My child could paint that." Ever heard that one in a museum? It's time to respond to this challenge. There have already been successful child painters who

Jean Dubuffet French Expressionist painter (1901–1985) who founded the movement known as *l'Art Brut* ("art in the raw," from which stems the modern-day concept of "outsider art") and whose interests lay in art exploration outside the aesthetic codes of the artistic elite, painting with thick, rough paint, and scratching into the paint's dry surface to typify this "truer," more primitive style.

made names for themselves as prodigies. In fact, I know a two-year-old whose drawings were accepted into a juried art show by curators who didn't suspect that he wasn't an adult. The unimpressed kid spent the entire art opening making sculptures out of the cheese cubes, just like a little art-star, but the real difference between the art of children and that of "professional" artists generally is that children make small drawings and paintings on the small sheets of paper we give them, while the pros make dramatic "works" on gargantuan canvases. That should be an easy trend to change.

YOU'LL NEED

The largest canvas you can afford
   (they come pre-stretched at art stores)
Paints and painting supplies
A child

So, for the "My Child Could Paint That" challenge, use the biggest canvas you can find and let the kid go for it on a large scale. Borrow someone else's kid if you don't have your own—these small creatures are not in short supply and you can find one pretty much anywhere you look.

You can set various parameters if you'd like to be sure of getting a contemporary masterpiece. For example, you might try painting the canvas all one color before you let the child loose, so you don't end up with too much white space—the hallmark of the amateur and something kids don't usually give much thought to. Or, limit the paint colors to only two choices so the kid can't turn everything into brown. You might try the child on only black and white for an interesting piece, or limit the child to other carefully chosen pairs: blue and yellow, for example.

Depending on the age of the child, you might get a lot of rocket ships and airplanes or flowers and stick figures. This is to be expected and well within the appropriate parameters of modern art. If you let your art prodigy glue some old baby clothes covered in mud to the canvas, you'll have something people might mistake for an original **Kiefer.** Or don't allow the use of any brushes. A huge canvas of handprints will instantly evoke **Marcus Harvey** and impress your guests, though they might get creeped out if they think about it too hard. Just don't forget to insist on a big, sloppy signature; this may be the art star of tomorrow—you never know.

Anselm Kiefer German Neo-Expressionist painter (b. 1945) known for his massive canvases, generally thickly textural and earthy-looking owing to his tendency to layer the paint with encrustations of anything from straw to . . . earth. The paintings tend to be somber and dramatic examinations of German postwar identity and culpability.

Marcus Harvey English painter (b. 1963) whose controversial 1995 painting of British child murderess Myra Hindley composed of tiny handprints is part of the Saatchi collection. The painting has been severely criticized and even "egged" by an offended British public.

"SEVEN YEARS' BAD LUCK" MIRROR

Breaking taboos is part of the Starving Artist's Way. Bypassing bourgeois constraints in favor of riotously unique living has always been a tenet of the bohemian life, though the reality is that artists come in all shapes and sizes. Sometimes they are the most straitlaced and conventional-seeming people, with completely normal "day jobs" and even full-fledged careers, like the New Jersey doctor/poet **William Carlos Williams.**

> **William Carlos Williams** American poet (1883–1963) who was a doctor in Rutherford, New Jersey, before becoming a poet. Williams greatly influenced the Beats and is the author of the epic poem of New Jersey, *Paterson.*

At any rate, a good way to exercise the ability to push your limits and break free of hampering rules is to actually break some stuff. And what better item to smash to bits than that quintessentially Eek-don't-break-it! item, the common wall mirror. You'll also feel very **Guerilla Girls** to be smashing one of the primary instruments of societal pressure we use to obsess over how we look.

> **Guerilla Girls**
> Anonymous group of media artists (founded 1985) who focus on issues of sexism and racism in the art world. They engage in humor-oriented vigilante tactics, usually pasting up posters and stickers, as well as cataloguing gender inequalities and lecturing on the subject, all while wearing big, goofy, creepy, hairy gorilla masks.

However, you must do the mirror smash-up with extreme care, as mirrors are made of glass—they are sharp and dangerous, probably the very attributes at the root of the taboo against breaking them. (Many taboos, such as those against procreating with a member of the immediate family or with an animal, are anchored in quite practical realities. I'll say no more as I'm sure you are getting my drift on this one.)

YOU'LL NEED
A mirror
Contact adhesive or tile glue
Tile grout
Safety wear and an old blanket

So, to be safe, take the mirror and wrap it well in an old blanket or rug that you will subsequently throw away. Put on sturdy work or gardening gloves and goggles. Lay the mirror on the ground and give it a good, swift smash with a hammer. Carefully unwrap to see what pieces your random act of violence has netted you, and then you can begin to plan the new design on your chosen surface. You can glue the mirror bits directly onto the wall, or you can create the whole project flat on a piece of plywood so it becomes portable, depending on your living situation. You can even cut the plywood to fit into a nice old frame, possibly a gold one with lots of little cherubs on it as is appropriate for a grand masterpiece. At any rate, keep your gloves on while you glue the chunks of mirror on your chosen surface, laying them out with small gaps of approximately ⅛ inch between each shard. You can also glue on bits of broken tile, plates, or other kinds of glass (good use for the beer bottle collection) between sections of mirror. When your area is completely filled, give it a chance to dry and then using grout, fill the gaps between the pieces to secure everything in place and to seal the sharp edges of the mirror shards.

The Velvet Underground Highly influential rock band founded in the early 1960s by Lou Reed and including John Cale, Sterling Morrison, and Maureen "Moe" Tucker. Created with support from Andy Warhol (before he lost interest), the infamous culture-maker provided the band with production help; gigs at his events such as the Exploding Plastic Inevitable; cover art for the record *The Velvet Underground and Nico* (1967); and even the singer Nico herself, whose heavy, Germanic vocals are typified by the song *I'll Be Your Mirror*.

And there you have your **Velvet Underground**-referencing "I'll Be Your Mirror" mosaic. The interestingly fragmented sense of self that is achieved by looking into this mirror can feel alternately **Cubistic,** schizophrenic, or like you're part of a piece by **Oscar Muñoz.** It's all in the eye of the beholder; whatever it is, it won't be boring.

Cubism A style of art that appeared in the 1910s that focused on displaying several aspects of an object or figure simultaneously. Noted practitioners of Cubism are the movement's creators Pablo Picasso (see page 40) and Georges Braque (see page 21).

Oscar Muñoz Colombian multimedia artist (b. 1951) who created a series of portraits painted so subtly onto mirrors with grease that they are visible only when the viewer breathes onto them. Not to be confused with Spanish sculptor Juan Muñoz (see page 44).

JAR-JUNK TIME CAPSULES

It's a strange phenomenon, the useless item we can't bring our-selves to part with: an old key, a bottle cap from some obscure brand of Caribbean beer, an expired driver's license, an old address book, a broken watch.... If you're going to keep this sort of clutter, it's time to bring it out into the light of day and show it off. Each one of these items might be junk on its own, but together, and with an influx of the spirit of **Joseph Cornell** and his fetish for preserving the small and ordinary, you can have a "collection."

The jar idea is something I got from my father, who has several on the shelves over his desk. He didn't in-vent the idea, however, but adapted it from a crafty guy in London who had giant jars like this in every room of his house. The method is simple.

Joseph Cornell American Surrealist assemblage/collage artist (1903–1972). The original outsider artist and mama's boy, Cornell lived his entire life in the family base-ment in Queens, New York, on the improbably named Utopia Parkway. His well-loved pieces consist of beautifully quiet and fetishistic compartmentalized wooden boxes housing small objects of all kinds.

YOU'LL NEED

Some of those industrial-size glass jars with the screw-on lids—the kinds you see in stores and restaurants that can hold a couple of gallons of pickled tomatoes or mayonnaise

Your collection of accumulated useless stuff

Sarah Sze   American installation artist (b. 1969) who creates complex, gravity-defying sculptural environments and wall pieces composed entirely of ordinary objects like teabags, houseplants, Q-tips, and extension cords.

Clean and dry the large jars thoroughly. Then start putting the little tchotchkes and whatchamacallits and thingymajiggies, and the bits of flotsam (or is it jetsam?), and also the things with names but no very apparent purpose into the jars. Just pack the stuff in. You don't need to fuss and plan over this one since you're not **Sarah Sze** here. When the jar's full, screw on the lid and move on to the next one. Line up your jars in a row somewhere, and enjoy the mesmerizing time capsule that you've created.

Friends and family will like to check out these jars and will periodically peer into the depths of one with the outraged exclamation "That's where that is! I've been looking all over for that!" which is, of course, what I always say to my father when I examine one of his jars. Of course, you could unscrew the lid and dump out the contents of the jar if necessary to get at and return the item in question (though my pops has not, to date, ever agreed to do it for me, so why should you?), but usually the kind of stuff that ends up in a junk jar will never genuinely be needed and you can always mumble some garbage about possession being so permeable and ephemeral and see if they just go away to study up on philosophy. The fact is that the junk is more useful this way—as a work of art. This project is your own personal exploration of what constitutes the matrix of the necessary and the profoundly unnecessary. Very deep, I know.

MODULAR BRANCHING LIGHT

A super-jazzy lighting idea for turning an overhead socket into an instant chandelier or for dressing up a standing lamp can be realized with just a minor assortment of electrical parts. The best thing about this project is its modular aspect, meaning you can grow or reconfigure it at any point, and it's a cheap and arty way to create an elaborate lighting fixture in a setting where you want something really modern and unusual. It exudes a bit of **Mona Hatoum,** too, which is pretty much priceless.

Mona Hatoum Lebanese-born Palestinian video, performance, and installation artist (b. 1952) whose work has included all kinds of lightbulbs, which are often contained in cages. Her video installation *Corps Étranger* (1994) was created by enlisting the aid of a medical doctor, and the resulting portrait of the artist includes such intimate and unconventional perspectives as that of a colonoscopy.

YOU'LL NEED

A central pre-existing socket to start, which can be an upright lamp or an overhead hanging fixture

As many socket "two-fers" as you want to use. These are socket branches that screw into an existing light bulb socket and create two sockets from the one (you can get these at Home Depot or an electrical-supply store)

There is an eventual limit to how extensively you'll want to branch this thing, as at a certain point you will begin to create weight, but anywhere up to 20 or so branches should be fine. Each socket screws into an earlier one, growing in any direction you choose. Bulbs then go in the available sockets. Use low-wattage night-light bulbs so as not to overload the pre-existing socket and cause a burn-out. Also, the smaller size of these

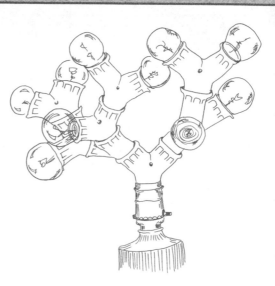

bulbs means you won't have the problem of bulbs butting against one another and cramping each other's space.

This can be a great piece to display during the winter holidays, as you can arrange one to hold eight bulbs and function as a flame-free menorah, while the combination of the plant-like branching form with the small decorative bulbs can grow into an ultra-mod, glowing tree for Christmas, too. All those bulbs give a quirky, **Rina Banerjee** installation effect, which you could maximize with the addition of some bits of colored cellophane or randomly placed umbrellas as decoration.

Rina Banerjee   Indian-born installation artist (b. 1963) who combines amusing with creepy to great effect, bringing together synthetic and natural elements like fake eyes, cellophane, rocks, and hair to create a paean to difference through quirky abstraction.

DETERGENT-BOTTLE WALL SCONCE

This idea for inexpensive mood lighting was conceived by painter Heidi Johnson. It's quirky and contemporary and 100 percent free—the perfect Starving Artist design. Also, laundry detergent bottles come in those crazy fluorescent shades, so the acidic pop colors with the translucent plastic steer clear of any potential hippie connotation that can attach themselves to many hand-crafted projects.

> **YOU'LL NEED**
>
> A large, empty plastic laundry detergent bottle
>   (around 100 ounces is a good size)
> Utility knife
> Screws

Take the bottle and rinse it well to get the residual soap out of it. By the way, if you don't have your own large bottle and you want to do this project, a quick perusal of the recycling bins at your local laundromat should provide you with the necessary raw materials.

Using a utility knife, cut down the sides of your bottle (see illustration), leaving a 1-inch-square tab sticking out on the middle of each side. Cut out the bottom of the bottle (note that the plastic here will be thicker and tougher to get through) and cut through the neck of the bottle, in line with the side seams. You may need a hacksaw to get through the spout portion, and if it's too difficult you can cut this piece off entirely, leaving your sconce straight across the bottom.

Feel free to leave any labels intact. These bottles, when illuminated, are super-bright and engaging, and they look good just as they are. I don't want to endorse any particular brand, but let's just say that orange is a nice color for these sconces as the light glows bright and fiery through the plastic. You can make small holes in the sconce by pressing and turning with the point of your knife or cut parts of the plastic out in any shapes you like for a **James Turrell** lighting effect.

James Turrell American installation artist (b. 1943) who plays with light and space and the activity of "seeing." Lives and works in Arizona at Roden Crater, an extinct volcano that he bought in the mid-1970s and in which he is building a large-scale environmental artwork and observatory.

Fold back the 1-inch tabs and screw them into the wall on either side of your light fixture. Make sure the bulb doesn't touch the plastic, otherwise you risk possible melting. If you have an exterior electrical cord powering your light fixture, let it run down the wall from the spout of the sconce, and it will look like it was meant to be there.

SILHOUETTE BOX LIGHT

Particularly at parties, but even just to keep yourself feeling party and cutting edge during your personal downtime, it's important to have some quirky and fun lighting effects around the house. Remember the incredible popularity of the Lava lamp? It practically defined a decade, after all. A clever combination of artiness and luminosity is not to be underestimated.

This cut-out, silhouette light box is a real beauty that is easy to put together and will cause the invitees to your next soiree to murmur awe-struck over your creativity (something every Starving Artist, calm and unconcerned as he or she may seem regarding the subject of external appreciation, is secretly hoping for).

YOU'LL NEED
2 pieces of clear plastic (Plexiglas), 1-foot square
Colored paper
4 12-inch squares of cardboard
Matte or X-Acto knife
Duct tape
Clip light

First, pick a design. It can be a grid of small squares, à la early **Frank Stella.** You can make a lightbulb shape—in a stylishly, self-referential nod to the fact that you are making a light—or if you have the requisite cutting skills, you can fill your page with lots of nineteenth-century silhouettes of pigtailed slave girls in pouffy dresses. I know, **Kara Walker** you are not, but you'll think of something. If you can cut it out, you can use it in this project.

Frank Stella American Minimalist painter and sculptor (b. 1936) who is credited with launching the Minimalist movement with his striped *Black Paintings* of the late 1950s. His work later evolved into his familiar brightly colored, sculptural, shaped canvases.

Kara Walker American installation artist (b. 1969) who uses the traditional Victorian art forms of the silhouette and the cyclorama to create elaborate and explicit images of Civil War–era Southern life, particularly grotesque images of slavery that peek from behind an ironically "quaint" veneer of Americana.

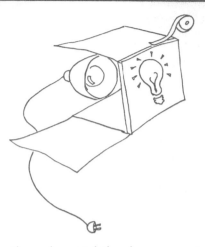

You can always trace a simple object like a splayed pair of scissors (you'll need to keep the cutouts of the finger holes and glue them back in place if you want this to look really good) or even some cookie-cutter stars.

Trace onto and cut the image out of colored paper, and sandwich the page between the pieces of plastic, taping around the edge. Lightly glue any cutout inserts, like the scissor holes, in place first. Then, tape together the sides of a box from the four pieces of cardboard and tape it behind the plastic (see drawing above). Leave the back open and stick a clip light inside. Sit the contraption on a shelf or in a corner somewhere, then switch it on and get groovy.

Alternatively, if you are too lazy to make this project, feel free to install some plain fluorescent tubes in various configurations and call it a **Dan Flavin** knock-off. Why not?

> **Dan Flavin**   American Minimalist sculptor (1933–1996) whose signature works were installations of ordinary fluorescent tubes in various colors.

CLOCKS FROM ANY OLD THING

You can make a clock out of anything on which you can mount clockworks. This means anything that you can drill a hole into and that's not thicker than a couple of inches so the clockworks can pass through—check out www.clockworks.com for inexpensive parts in varying sizes and the instructions to attach them. Basically, the motor needs to go on the back of your chosen clock face and the hands on the front, and there's a rod that joins the two (the shank) that passes through the hole you've made. That's pretty much the whole story of the clock, and you do not need any enraptured-with-the-machine explanatory drawings by **Francis Picabia** to understand it.

You can make numbers on your clock or not—if you're old enough

> **Francis Picabia**
> French Dadaist/Surrealist painter (1879–1953) who was included in and actually showed up for the famous Armory Show that caused such a stir back in 1913 in New York. His *Mechanical Drawings* combined the technical with the figurative, and display his pre-apocalyptic vision that the machine is the source of all human life.

to read this sentence, you no doubt have a pretty good sense of where those numbers go even when they're not there. If you can't entirely decide, you can make a clock out of a metal disk, such as an old circular-saw blade, and stick on refrigerator magnet numbers. You can switch the numbers around occasionally, or remove entirely to befuddle self and family. This is a particularly dastardly and fun game to play on kids who are just learning to tell time—it toughens 'em up for the cold, cruel world. You can use all number 5s, dusted with metallic spray paint, for a reference to **Charles Demuth**'s *I Saw the Figure 5 in Gold.* You can also use numbers in various funky fonts that you find on paper or print out from the Web and decoupage them onto your clock surface.

The base of your clock can be pretty much anything, but just make sure you get the appropriate drill bit for the center hole, as they come made especially for wood, metal, glass, and tile, etc. Measure the diameter of the shank and get the right-size bit. If you are drilling into metal, you should start by making an indentation with a hammer and nail, so your drill bit has someplace to settle into. Otherwise you'll find it skids around and it's hard to get the hole started.

Some possible designs: Try a saw blade or hubcap clock. Or, as a tribute to the broken crockery king of the 1980s, **Julian Schnabel,** and as a way to do something with an otherwise useless smashed dish, you can make a nice clock out of an unfortunately busted-up plate.

YOU'LL NEED

A plate

Clockworks (try your local hardware store or
    www.clockworks.com)

Appropriate size ceramic drill bit and power drill

Cardboard

Matte knife

White epoxy

Spray glue

Paint for stencils

If you happen to have dropped your favorite plate, you should use that one. If you need to break a plate specifically for the project, buy one at a thrift store. Wrap it in an old blanket, wear goggles and work gloves, and smash the bundle with a hammer. You can also, of course, just drop it on your kitchen floor, loudly yell "Oh damn!" and then carefully pick up all the pieces, trying not to cut yourself in a theatrical reenactment of one of life's many frustrating momentary dramas. Only kidding. Don't do it that last way. Do it the other way with the blanket and all the safety stuff.

Handling the broken plate pieces carefully, rearrange them and glue them back together with the epoxy. Leave out some small chips and chunks for a look that boldly says "broken plate" as long as the plate can still hold together. Try to keep it solid in the center to support the clockworks, and around the rim so it won't be dangerous to handle.

Make a mark in the plate's center, and using your drill bit made for ceramic or tile, drill a hole all the way through. Attach the clock motor to the back and the hands to the front of the clock. The clockworks should have instructions showing you how and in what order to attach the various pieces, but it's not complicated.

You can paint on stenciled numbers for this clock, or glue on small flattish objects in place of numbers. To make a stencil, type the numbers 1–12 on your computer in a font that doesn't use circles, such as FuturaBlack BT, or copy these:

1 2 3 4 5 6 7 8 9 10 11 12

Notice how the numbers look a lot like the text in a **Christopher Wool** painting? With this font, you can cut out each piece of a number (look at the 4, 6, 8, 9, and 0) without having any center pieces that fall out. This is the key to an effective stencil. Size the font to at least 36, probably bigger if you have a large plate; make sure there's plenty of space between the numbers, and print them out.

> **Christopher Wool**   American painter (b. 1955) best known for stenciled paintings of phrases culled from pop culture and awkwardly broken across the surface of the canvas.

Spray-mount the numbers smoothly to thin cardboard (from a cereal or shoe box) and cut around each one with a craft knife to create the stencil opening. Mark the placement for each number around the edge of your clock and lay the first number stencil in place. Mask off any other exposed parts of the clock with paper and spray lightly through the number, or use a small amount of acrylic paint and a dry brush, making sure to hold the stencil firmly and fill the entire opening. Carefully lift the stencil away in one movement, without shifting to avoid smudging.

Hang the clock on the wall or put on a shelf. Check out how this new tool aids you in your awareness of planetary progress around the solar center of our galactic system. You will be able to locate yourself in that process, as well as coordinate your movements with those of other entities by the use of this mind-bogglingly ingenious device. It's very handy. I would recommend one of these "clock" things for anybody who has places to go and people to see. If you are content to live alone in a cave, I suspect you won't be needing one and in that case, carry on as you were.

COVER-UP CARPET SQUARES

Being a true Starving Artist requires rolling with a few unexpected punches. Here's a test: Whoops. Stained the carpet. Just like in one of those TV commercials for paper towels. Now what do you do?

How'd you answer? Well, don't freak out and rearrange all the furniture or, worse still, recarpet the entire room. If **Joseph Albers** were here he'd design an artful square inside a square pattern that would completely transform the offending area and make you love your messed-up carpet even more than the original. Joseph Albers is, of course, not here. Instead he's busy rolling around in his grave at the idea that I mentioned his name in my frivolous book and haven't addressed any of the important principles of modern design. Oh well. Sorry, Joe.

Joseph Albers
German-born Op Art painter and designer (1888–1976) who was an instructor at the Bauhaus School before emigrating to America, where he taught for many years at Black Mountain College and at Yale, helping to educate lots of the important postwar American artists. His own most famous work is a series of precise color experiments best explained by his own title as *Homage to the Square*.

YOU'LL NEED

Carpet square

Straight edge

Chalk

Utility knife

Carpet tape

Get a bit of carpet remnant or a small mat of a color that will look splashy with your existing floor covering—a similar thickness is the more usual choice, but a square of shag might look outrageously good. Just pick a nicely complementary color. Using a straight edge for neatness, mark out a chalk square around the area of the carpet you need to remove and cut it out with a sharp knife. Lay the cut-out bit back-to-back on your remnant and trace the size of the square.

Cut the remnant to size and, using carpet tape, affix to the floor with the ends tucked under the edges of the opening. Place the new, different-colored square of carpet in the place of the old and marvel at the introduction of inspirational recklessness into your life. Put a weight on the new section for several hours to seal it down. Or if you feel really adventurous, just cover the spot with a small **cairn** and call it sculpture.

Cairn   One friend of mine circled this word when reading through a draft of the book, asking me to include a sidebar definition. I'm very sorry about that, but I refuse to do it. Look it up in the dictionary, for god's sake! I can't be explaining every word that you don't know—that's what *Webster's* is for, and it's a really great resource for all kinds of confusing and/or unfamiliar terms.

RACQUET PHOTO FRAME

Badminton is back. Well, not as a game. At least, I hadn't noticed it returning as a game and I wouldn't be mentioning it here if it was. After all, this is not *The Starving Artist's Guide to Retro Lawn and Parlor Games.* Badminton is back in the sense that we are going to put to good use all those racquets you see floating through junk shops, garages, yard sales, attics. If you're **Jessica Stockholder,** of course, you've probably already figured out a way to put them to use, so never mind. The rest of you might as well read on.

> **Jessica Stockholder** American installation artist (b. 1959) who creates her work from arrangements of ordinary objects like tennis balls and cans of paint in juxtapositions designed to elicit new meanings and perceptions.

It's a pretty oddball moniker, "badminton," though not even remotely as bizarre as "shuttlecock," which is the name for the thing you're supposed to hit around with the badminton racquet. The very idea of badminton is kind of classically British in spirit—reminiscent of P. G. Wodehouse characters getting out of "scrapes" with the help of clever valets not weighed down by years of aristocratic inbreeding and lazing about. And those cucumber sandwiches with the crusts cut off. And people playing sports in white V-necked sweaters. And **Lucian Freud** and **YBAs** and ... OK, wow,

> **Lucian Freud** German-born English Neo-Expressionist painter (b. 1922). Freud's focus on portraiture, and particularly the seemingly blank and alienated mood that is expressed with his figures, has caused all kinds of speculation about the role of psychology in his work, and in particular the possible legacy of granddaddy Sigmund, aka the father of modern psychoanalysis.

YBAs   An abbreviation for the term Young British Artists, coined by advertising mogul/art collector Charles Saatchi and including Damien Hirst, Rachel Whiteread, Chris Ofili, and Tracey Emin.

I'm digressing. Let's just say that if you've got one or two of those badminton racquets and you don't know what to do with them, here's an idea.

The racquets are nice objects and are generally made of wood, which is always rustic and charming, and are equipped with nice round openings, a perfect Starving Artist–styled picture frame. You can paint the racquet first if you want, or give it a coat of shiny polyurethane. Cut out the strings so you will be able to see your picture clearly—unless you are truly and deeply arty and want to make a point about how the human condition is one of bondage and we all live caged lives. Then, by all means go ahead and mount your photo behind that mesh of strings.

YOU'LL NEED

The racquet

A photo

A sheet of light cardboard (the cereal box type is fine)

Pencil

X-Acto knife

Tape

A small piece of wire

Wood glue

Paint, decorative paper, spray mount (all optional)

Take the cardboard and trace around the face of the racquet. Cut out the cardboard oval and trim to fit exactly on the back of the racquet without sticking out on the sides. You can paint this cardboard or spray-mount nice paper to it, as this will be the "matte" for your photo.

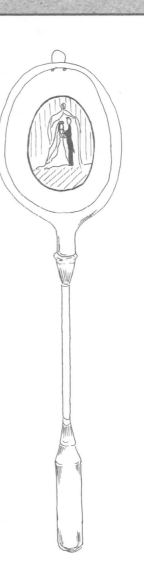

Now, decide on the size of your matte window. It should be smaller than your photo so the photo's edges don't show, but how much smaller is negotiable. Let's say ½ inch all around. Cut the center of the cardboard with a knife to create an opening that is 1 inch less than your photo in both length and width, and tape your photo to the back of this opening. Glue the cardboard to the back of the racquet. Attach a small loop of wire through the top two string holes in the racquet and hang your photo on the wall. Presto and voilà. You can also cross a pair of these racquets, wiring their handles together in the middle, for "doubles" pictures where you have two photos that go together well.

DADA PHOTO FRAME

This picture frame is one that can be made out of pretty much anything. In fact, the more nonsensical, the better if you want to achieve the true **Dada** spirit. **Kurt Schwitters,** the master of this sort of thing, would make ample use of old ticket stubs and other scraps of paper, but you are welcome to use something zingier, if you like. You could do a **Romare Bearden** street scene or just use bits of color and shape. Old cartons with bright imagery can work well, as can strictly black and white, **John Baldessari**-type collages.

Kurt Schwitters German Dadaist artist (1887–1948) who referred to his own less political brand of Dadaism as "Merz," a syllable he lifted from a snipped bit of found paper. Schwitters constructed collages out of scraps and refuse, and built assemblage sculptures that eventually filled up his entire house, poking through floors and ceilings.

Dadaism An aesthetic movement that began in Zurich and in New York in 1919 as a reaction to the violence and pointlessness of World War I. The name means "hobby-horse" in French, and Dadaism is correspondingly characterized by irrationality, nonsense, and the rejection of established values. Noted practitioners are Marcel Duchamp, Max Ernst, Man Ray, and Kurt Schwitters.

Romare Bearden American Monumental Realist collage artist (1911–1988) who created numerous cut-and-paste scenes of African-American life and was strongly influenced by his exposure to and interest in jazz.

John Baldessari American conceptual artist (b. 1931). Known for his series of humorous black-and-white collages, as well as jokey text paintings on the subject of art and art history.

YOU'LL NEED

A photo
Collaging images
Cardboard
Matte knife
Duct tape
White or wood glue
Clear packing tape

Measure your photo. Add 4 inches to the length and width, and cut 2 pieces of cardboard to this size. This will give you 2 inches all around your photo. One piece of cardboard is the back, so you can leave it simple or cover it with paper. For the front piece, you need to cut out an opening in the center—make it 1 inch smaller than your photo in both length and width and centered, so you'll have a ½-inch cover around the edges of the image. Tape the two pieces of cardboard together on three sides with duct tape, leaving the top open to slide your photo in and out.

Take your collage elements and glue them onto the border of the frame. If they are cut from cardboard, they can protrude slightly into the opening and off the edge of the frame for a more dynamic look; otherwise, you'll need to glue them to thin cardboard first and then to the frame, so they don't flop over. Now, for the magic: Take clear packing tape and lay it neatly over the surface of your collage to laminate it, slightly overlapping each piece until the whole thing is covered (you may be surprised how nice this can look if done neatly). Let the edges wrap around onto the back and through the opening to secure them. Smooth out any wrinkles, and cut out any tape that protrudes into your picture opening.

Make a 3-inch-wide strip of cardboard of the same height as your frame and tape the end of it securely onto the back of your frame about 2 inches below the top. This creates a hinge, so you can make the frame stand. Slide the photo into the frame so it shows through the opening. If the packing tape looks too wrinkly and you don't like it, just try to think of it as **"outsider art"** and you will start to feel better and somehow "cutting edge" right away.

> **Outsider Art** A phrase used since the 1970s to refer to artwork that is made outside the domain of fine art by people who may be mentally ill or otherwise unable to comply with cultural norms, although loose usage has seen it referring to simply untrained or unconnected artists. (I do it myself in this book.)

PACK-RAT PAPER NOTEBOOK

Having a book in your back pocket or bag for "taking notes" is an important tool of the Starving Artist. This is not, however it may seem, merely an affectation, especially if, like me, you are working on a book and you never know at what random time an idea may strike you that will need to be jotted down quickly so as not to be forgotten. Even if you are not writing a book, you never know at what random time an opportunity to write a book may strike you that will require all those notes.

YOU'LL NEED

Paper for the interior
Cardboard for the covers
Binder clip
Utility knife
Power drill
Wire or string to attach

Keep a stash of odd sheets of paper until you have enough for this project, though you might want to hide them so people don't grab them off your stack **Felix Gonzalez-Torres**-style. You can make it a true recycled notebook if you use pages with text on

Felix Gonzalez-Torres

Cuban installation artist (1957–1996) who created works inviting audience participation through innocently seductive means as in *Untitled (Placebos)*, which offered the public free candy from a heap on the floor, and *Untitled (The End)*, which consisted of a stack of paper, sheets of which were made available for the taking.

one side, and make yours a one-sided notebook. Some different-colored papers are fun to add for an occasional perky moment. If you have access to a copy store where you can use the paper cutter, take your sheets in and trim them to the size you've chosen for your book. Otherwise, cut them with a matte knife or scissors, a few sheets at a time. This will make for a more rustic book, but it still works fine if you go about it neatly and carefully. For the cover you can use cardboard, an old hardcover from a book, or a section of an unused and spiffy game board.

Cut the cover to size with your utility knife to the same dimensions as the pages. Then, using a binder clip, clamp the covers with the pages between and drill 3 holes along one edge, about ½ inch in and evenly spaced. You can attach it all together with binder rings, ribbon, string, or wire, but make sure to leave it loose enough for the pages to turn freely without ripping.

For the front cover, if it's undecorated, you can make a stencil of your name or the word BOOK (stick on vinyl letters, spray-paint over them, and then peel them back off in the style of Ed Ruscha, page 25) or cut an opening in the front cover for a window. Glue a piece of clear acetate behind the opening so you can write or draw something on the first page to be seen through the window. The voyeur "peeping tom" vibe reminds me of the second-best **Michael Powell** (without

Michael Powell and Emeric Pressburger

English/Hungarian filmmaking team who worked in the 1940s and 50s as "The Archers" and co-credited themselves as writer, director, and producer, although supposedly Powell actually did the directing and Pressburger the writing. *The Red Shoes* (1948) is their best-known movie. Powell made *Peeping Tom* (1960) after the partnership split, and both the film and Powell himself owe some continued popularity to Martin Scorsese, who has repeatedly cited it as an influence.

his sometime partner-in-crime **Emeric Pressburger**) movie. The jury's still out on which is the first best, although that bizarre plot about the guy who pours glue on girls' heads has the relatively unknown *A Canterbury Tale* running strong, in my opinion.

BUBBLE GUM MARBLEIZED ACCESSORIES

basic tenet of the Starving Artist's Way is to transform unwanted refuse into a thing of beauty. This is partly because unwanted refuse is generally free and abundant. This is partly because the Starving Artist appreciates the challenge of turning "nothing" into "something." Gold, for example, is considered intrinsically valuable even when it's only in the form of unsightly little lumps, but when **Chris Ofili** paints his beautiful psychedelic swirls on a canvas smeared with elephant dung, you know it's got to be his artistic prowess that creates the value, not the raw materials.

Chris Ofili British contemporary painter (b. 1968). Ofili's intricate and colorful paintings reference aspects of contemporary black life using pop stereotypes, traditional African imagery, and even elephant excrement collected from the London Zoo as part of the process.

Carl Andre American Minimalist sculptor (b. 1935) known for floor pieces, generally squares of industrial materials (metal, bricks, etc.) laid out in various horizontal configurations.

Anyone who lives in a city (except Singapore, where it's against the law to chew gum) is familiar with that ubiquitous sidewalk patterning of flattened and gray-toned chewing-gum circles. There's an interesting **Carl Andre**-meets-**Ross**

Ross Bleckner American painter (b. 1949), whose paintings have been read as AIDS-era elegies and portray the spiritual and the architectural via copious dots and stripes and moody colors.

Bleckner effect of squashed underfoot **Pointillism** if you've got an imagination and aren't too easily grossed out. However, let's face it, few of us wax analytical over the sight of smushed chewing gum that's been trodden over.

Pointillism A French school of painting (ca. 1880) considered an outgrowth of Impressionism. Pointillism as a concept consisted of making small dots of paint that appear to blend from a distance. Georges Seurat and Camille Pissarro both favored this technique.

Let's learn to love chewed gum: Bubble gum comes in beautiful shades of pink and purple, and its uniquely rubbery consistency is perfect for making marbleized surfaces like coasters or place mats. The super-ambitious might try a tabletop, especially if you happen to have an army of chewers at your disposal.

YOU'LL NEED
Oaktag or thin cardboard
Lots of chewed gum
Clear varnish
Hairdryer
Utility knife

Cut your piece of oaktag or cardboard to the size of the project you want to make or the surface you want to cover, adding an extra ¼ inch in each direction. Place in a convenient spot for collecting gum. As you finish chomping on your grape or watermelon Bubble Yum (or whatever), just stick it onto the cardboard and flatten it with your fingers. Stick the next piece beside the first, allowing the edges to touch or even slightly overlap. Put different colors next to each other. As you fill the area, press the gum bits flat and toward each other, smoothing the surface with your fingers.

When you've got all your gum in place, you may need to run a hairdryer lightly over the surface to soften the mass, and then with dampened fingers (to minimize sticking), gently push the different colors into each other to create a marbleized effect. Don't work the gum surface too ferociously or you'll thin it out, but should you happen to cause a hole, just patch it with another piece of gum. When your surface is smooth, allow it to harden for a day. Coat the gum with clear-gloss varnish to protect it.

Trim the ¼-inch border of excess oaktag or cardboard with your utility knife and simply place the mat on your chosen surface.

Be prepared for some softening in hot weather (it's gum, remember?), though the varnish coating will prevent it from becoming sticky. This makes a great conversation piece. It has a delicate fruity smell, which some people will really enjoy and others, well, won't. Too bad for them. Just babble something about **John Waters** and Odorama. Or the naysayers might be impressed by a reference to **Richard Artschwager** and the idea of using "fake" materials of one kind to simulate another.

John Waters American filmmaker (b. 1946) and favorite son of the city of Baltimore. Waters makes films that are good-naturedly gross and campy, including *Hairspray* (1988), starring a young Ricki Lake and transvestite Divine as her mother. Waters created "Odorama" for his 1981 film *Polyester*, an idea which consisted of scratch 'n sniff cards corresponding to on-screen numbers and offering such delectable aromas as dog shit.

Richard Artschwager American Pop/conceptual artist (b. 1923) who enjoys tricks of perception as in *Door* (1990), surfaced with Formica, patterned to look like wood.

DECOUPAGE PLACE MATS

Decoupage is a great trick for decorating anything that has a solid surface. Of course, it's not even really a "trick" since it refers only to gluing paper cut-outs onto something, and people have been doing it for centuries because it's so darn easy and obvious.

Avoid shiny papers, which may curl up. You can make a color copy of any image you like and use that—so you can keep special originals to use again and again. Cut out the images and glue them down, pressing smooth to avoid trapping air bubbles, and then when dry, seal over for protection with a thin brushing of polyurethane. Crack a window so you don't get woozy from the smell, and allow the polyurethane to dry according to instructions.

YOU'LL NEED

Images to decoupage
A sheet of colored oaktag (11 × 17 inches makes a good size)
Clear contact paper
Scissors
White or wood glue

#1 low-budget method A decoupage place mat can be made by gluing the images directly onto the oaktag and then covering the front and back with a sheet of clear contact paper. You'll want to lay out the contact paper and place your decorated mat facedown onto the sticky side, with a border of contact paper all around. Stick a sheet of contact paper onto the back and allow the edges to stick together, enveloping your mat inside. Trim the edges to about ¼ inch of contact-to-contact seal. A note about the "less-slick" method: This is not necessarily inferior. Homemade is good. It's just a question of allowing things to have quirky charm and understanding your own particular skill set.

#2 slicker, not-quite-as-cheap method Decoupage onto any size paper you like. Take the finished piece to the copy store and have it blown up to 11 × 17 inches and copied as many times as you like to make a set. Then laminate your mats at the store for a smooth, protected finish.

Note You can find tons of flower images in magazines and old books, and they look good when you just cram them in, overlapping them into a dense garden of flora. You can use generic images or find snippets of **O'Keeffe** paintings or **Mapplethorpe** photos (the flowers, in this case, not the naked guys, unless you have a racy image of the place mats you'd like at dinner).

Georgia O'Keeffe American Modernist painter (1887–1986) of mostly close-up interiors of flowers (which have, in spite of her objections, been inevitably perceived as having sexual connotations) as well as old cow skulls and other features of the American Southwestern landscape.

Robert Mapplethorpe American photographer (1946–1989) and recipient of a controversial government grant that prompted Jesse Helms to throw his hat into the ring against the NEA in the 1980s. Mapplethorpe created almost classically perfect images of naked men often with explicit props and positions connoting gay sex acts. He is also known for an arguably more chaste series of close-up photos of flowers.

HOMEMADE PILLOWCASES AND DRAPES

A pillowcase is an envelope of fabric that's almost invariably 21 inches wide by 30 inches long, so if you can sew a straight seam, you can make a pillowcase. It's that simple. What homemade pillowcases offer you is the opportunity to add *accent* or *spice*, the favorite buzz-concepts of home decorating magazines, to a fairly inexpensive bedding collection. To create a full bedding ensemble, cut an additional square of the new pillowcase fabric and stitch it flat onto the lower left quadrant of the surface of your top sheet to *tie in* the different-colored pieces. Or be daring with a **Ghada Amer** reference and some risqué decorative stitchery on the pillowcases and the sheet.

Ghada Amer Egyptian-born contemporary artist (b. 1963) whose brightly colored canvases have made a big splash owing to their almost abstract-looking, stitched shapes, which on close inspection turn out to be graphic images of women taken from pornographic magazines.

YOU'LL NEED
Appropriate fabric (see below)
Scissors
Needle and thread

To create the pillowcase, cut a rectangle from any washable fabric that measures 43 by 31 inches. Hem one of the 43-inch lengths by folding over ½ inch onto the wrong side of the fabric and sewing flat. This keeps the edge from getting frayed and ragged. Fold the piece in half the long way still wrong side out and sew a seam along the 31-inch length about ½ inch from the edge. Close the raw end of the sleeve with a seam and turn right side out. Done.

Note This is certainly easiest to do on a sewing machine, but if you don't have one, just sit in front of the TV and sew the seams by hand. It won't kill you. In fact, it might be a good opportunity to turn a video camera on yourself and do a multimedia piece. Or just get in the groove and feel quilty, like **Faith Ringgold.**

> **Faith Ringgold** American mixed media and performance artist (b. 1930) best known for her "storytelling quilts" of the 1970s. She is also the author of numerous children's books containing quilted imagery. Her first, *Tar Beach,* is still the most famous. See another artist's vision of Ringgold herself in the 1976 painting by the incomparably quirky portraitist Alice Neel (1900–1984).

Curtains or drapes are just as easy, and can be made to match the bed sheets if you'd like to further *tie in* your linens. Cut a piece of fabric the height of your window plus 6 inches and the width of your window plus 16 inches (the additional width is to allow draped folds to form). Hem all the edges. Fold the top end 3 inches down and stitch across the curtain. Thread a curtain rod through this sleeve and hang your new curtain. You can make two separate curtains, in which case cut the fabric for each panel 10 inches more than half your window's width. You can make full drapes the same way, adjusting the length to reach the floor.

ARSONIST'S TABLECLOTHS

Ruination! Maybe you have an old tablecloth that's been "destroyed" by a stain? Or maybe there's a beautiful relic going cheap at the Salvation Army for the same reason? Don't sweat it and don't throw anything away, because you can make your own, good-as-new, **Willie Cole**-inspired tablecloth with nothing more than an iron and an at-the-ready fire extinguisher (!).

YOU'LL NEED

A tablecloth

An iron

Willie Cole American sculptor (b. 1955) who works largely with discarded domestic items, including irons. His pieces evoke visual relationships between the marks of the different irons and African tribal masks.

The basic idea for this project is to set up your cloth on an ironing board and leave the iron on just long enough to make a brown "burn" mark. This is exactly the thing you would normally try to avoid doing if you were living an ordinary existence and not that of a daring Starving Artist. If you make the burn marks into patterned shapes (they could be the petals of a large flower), you can create something really beautiful and unique that becomes a work of art rather than a scene of domestic bliss gone awry. You can create beautiful, soft beige-y patterns by leaving a hot iron in one place for about 15 seconds. You can combine this with a deeper brown color if you leave it for 25 seconds, but be careful about leaving it too much longer—at a certain point you'll start to burn through the fabric and you'll need that fire extinguisher we talked about earlier, as well as a good explanation for the fire department and/or any roommates you may have.

Different irons have different shapes and designs and you can use that to your advantage in planning your pattern. Of course, burning things is a dangerous activity so you need to keep your eye on this project at all times. Try to stick to fabrics made of cotton and other natural fibers to avoid the plastic-y and probably carcinogenic fumes of burning synthetics.

It you are really adventurous with your burning, like **Yves Klein,** you can try a different project: burn small holes all over a tablecloth and lay it over a cloth of a different color for a nice effect. If you do freeform burning like this, do it outside and keep some water handy for dousing the project if your burns get out of hand. Also, make sure your work area is completely clear of any papers or other fabrics that could catch the blaze, and that you yourself are not wearing loose clothing and that all hair is tucked away. Pull your hair back like a schoolmarm; this is not the time for the Rapunzel look.

The simplest method for burning is to lay out your cloth and then pull up peaks in the fabric at intervals. Light these peaks on fire one at a time with a match or lighter, blowing them out as soon as

Yves Klein French conceptual artist (1928–1962) best known for his monochrome paintings and the particular shade of pigment he termed "Yves Klein Blue." Klein is also remembered fondly for the fact that he used naked models as brushes with which to apply paint (by ordering them to roll on the canvas) and for his torched "fire paintings," which look unmistakably like canvases that have been mottled and browned with the tongue of a flame.

they catch the flame. Every time an area looks like it needs a burn, tug the fabric up into a peak in that spot and light it up. Be careful; while an arsonist might tell you that fire itself is an art form—and that inner pyromaniac of yours might be tempted to agree—I don't want you burning your house down and then saying I told you to do it. I most definitely did *not* tell you to do it. Proceed at your own risk.

HOT GLUE LACE TABLE-CLOTH OR PLACE MATS

Hot glue is an amazing substance. It's not that it creates the strongest of bonds, or that it's the most invisible. It's not even the simplest glue to work with. In fact, it introduces the potential hazard of "the burn" to the activity of gluing. What's particularly great about hot glue, however, is its open-endedness. It's easy to handle, being dispensed via a "gun," which also makes it more fun to use than other tubey or squirty glues, and it dries extremely rapidly, which enables you to work quickly and feel very efficient. Furthermore, hot glue doesn't pack the toxic punch of most of the powerful glues. Best of all, it has a nifty, rubbery quality, which you can use for unorthodox projects like the hot glue ideas in this book. A hot glue gun will run you only a few bucks at hardware or craft stores, and it's an indispensable tool.

Finding new and unusual ways to work with ordinary materials is one of the routes Starving Artists take to expand the possibilities of their limited resources. Furthermore, this idea is great for all those situations where you want a doily kind of item to place under something, but don't want to feel as fussy and old-fashioned as your grandmother. Of course, lace textures are being explored as art in their own right by such current artists as **Anne Wilson,** so your grand-mother might reasonably ask "Who's more hip than who?" or even "Who's more hip than whom?" if your grandma happens to have a particular knack for the intricacies of English grammar.

YOU'LL NEED
Pages from magazines, preferably brightly colored
Hot glue gun and several sticks of glue

Depending on what size piece you'd like to create, lay out one or several magazine pages, slightly overlapping, to fill your work area. Take your hot glue gun and, from about 4 to 6 inches away, allow the glue to flow onto the papers, keeping the gun moving back, forth, and around to make random, lacy patterns. Keep the work fairly dense. Most gaps between glue strands should be no more than ½ inch apart. When the area is filled, allow the piece just a few seconds to dry completely and then peel it off the magazine pages. The bits of color and imagery that are stuck to the glue will stay—any bits of paper between need to be ripped away. You can be as perfectionist about this as you want. Some extremely thin glue strands will break in the clean-up process and can be pulled off and forgotten about.

Anne Wilson American conceptual artist (b. 1949) working primarily with found textiles and fiber crafts. Her well-known *Topologies* is an installation of dissected black lace. She has made a series of projects stitched from human hair.

Use a large piece of hot glue lace as a see-through overlay on top of a plain tablecloth, or make mats or coasters to serve any purpose.

MINI(MALIST) CUBE PICTURE FRAME

Yep, another picture frame. This one is exceptionally sharp, with a Minimalist vibe—good for a black-and-white, **Man Ray**-type artfully dramatic close-up. Or for anything else you might want. I'm not here to tell you what to do, but this idea turns out really well if you make several tiny versions of these cubes and use them to display groups of photos from a photo-booth strip.

Man Ray American Dadaist/Surrealist photographer, collage/assemblage artist (1890–1976), and great pal of Marcel Duchamp. Ray began as a commercial fashion photographer and went on to create some of the classic images of early-twentieth-century art photography, such as *Tears* (1932–33) and the woman recast as an instrument *Le Violon d'Ingres* (1924).

YOU'LL NEED

A photo

2 squares of clear Plexiglas of at least 1–2-inch thickness and any height and width you like as long as they are identical and as big as or larger than your photo; to make a cube that will easily stand, the height/width of each square should be twice its thickness

Black duct tape or clear packing tape

Slide your photo between the two squares and run a neat line of tape around the edge, sealing the photo in, and locking the two Plexi slabs to each other.

Unless you want to spend your last dollar on Plexiglas, you should stick with small photos for this project. There is no room for a full-size **Gursky** here—or for that matter, anyone else from the **Düsseldorf School**. In fact, it's a great way to add substance to a really tiny photo of only 2 or 3 inches, and turn it into a satisfying object. You can make a couple of different-size cubes and stack them like blocks. Each photo becomes its own cube, and they function together as a stackable set. It's so sleek and modern.

Andreas Gursky
German photographer (b. 1955) known for his slick, mammoth images (some over 15 feet in length) generally juxtaposing mass commerce with individual insignificance.

Düsseldorf School
In contemporary lingo, this refers to the popular German photographers from the last few decades who studied under Bernd and Hilla Becher at the Kunstakademie in Düsseldorf, Germany. This group includes Andreas Gursky, Thomas Struth, Candida Hofer, and Thomas Ruff. Technically, of course, artists have studied in Düsseldorf for centuries, but these days it'd be a safe bet that if somebody's talking about the Düsseldorf School, that person isn't talking about the old dead guys.

CASSETTE TAPE DOORWAY CURTAIN

Still got a bunch of those old cassette tapes lying around? Well, if you threw them out last week, you're about to get all sad and sorry that in the interests of saving space you blew your chance of doing this project. Lucky for you, cassette tapes can still be found in the back corner of almost any old junk shop, so you've no excuse for not making this beauteous home adornment.

Magnetic tape is a versatile thing. In fact, just ask **Christian Marclay**—he crocheted a pillow out of the complete works of the Beatles on audiotape. If you know how to crochet or knit, you can go nuts with the stuff. If you don't, or don't have the time, stick with this quick and easy project.

Christian Marclay

American conceptual artist, musician, and "turntablist" (b. 1955) who examines the connection between the visual and the audible via the playing of broken and reconstituted records, distorting instruments into unplayable sculptures and numerous other experiments in sound.

YOU'LL NEED

A dozen or more old audiocassette tapes (or try video!)
Black duct tape
Scissors
Staple gun or grommets

Measure the width of your chosen doorway and lay a strip of duct tape, sticky side up, onto the edge of a table. Make it a little longer than the doorway's width so you have room to tape down each end of this piece of tape to your table or you will find it impossible to maneuver. Snip the tape where it comes out of the cassette so you have

a free end, and stick
this end to the duct
tape. Pull the tape out
of the cassette by gently walking backwards
with the cassette in
hand until it's the approximate length of
your doorway's height.
You can cut strips a bit
shorter to keep them

from dragging on the floor and catching dirt. Snip the cassette free
and start a new strip. Put the tape ends as close together as you can,
even overlapping slightly so the curtain won't be too thin.

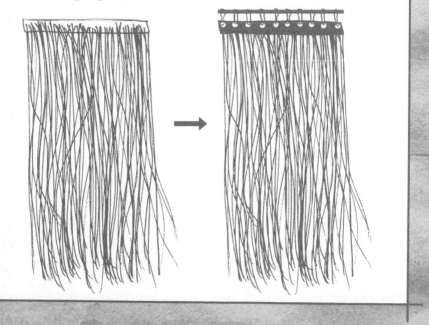

When you've filled the whole piece of duct tape with tape strips, lay another strip of tape (sticky side down) across it, sealing all the ends. Trim to the doorway width using your trusty scissors. You can grommet some holes in the duct tape, use a hole-punch, or just staple it up to the doorframe. The tape will glint and shimmer in the light, especially if you have a breeze, and it feels silky smooth when you walk through it. You will love it or your money back. Not really.

The one major problem I can see with the explanation for this project is that it involves a confusing multiple use of the word *tape* to refer to magnetic tape and sticky tape, as well as to the verb *to tape*. I tried to be careful with my language, but short of making up dorky synonyms like "adhesive strip," this was the best I could do. In the interests of clarity, we'll try using the following code to simplify the instructions for the confused among you:

The word *bumpkin* will refer to *magnetic tape*.
The word *swizzle* will refer to *duct tape*.
The word *ameliorate* will refer to *tape*, the verb.

Got it? Remember, please, that this is going to hurt me much more than it is going to hurt you, though fans of **language poetry** will probably even like it.

OK, let's try:

Measure the width of your chosen doorway and lay a strip of swizzle, sticky side up, onto the edge of a table. Make it a little longer than the doorway's width so you have room to ameliorate down each end of this piece of swizzle to your table, or you will find it impossible to maneuver.

Snip the bumpkin where it comes out of the cassette so you have a free end, and stick this end to the swizzle. Pull the bumpkin out of the cassette by gently walking backwards with the cassette in hand until it's the approximate length of your doorway's height. You can cut strips a bit shorter to keep them from dragging on the floor and catching dirt. Snip the cassette free and start a new strip. Put the bumpkin ends as close together as you can, even overlapping slightly so the curtain won't be too thin. Are these instructions beginning to sound like the score for a **John Cage** evening? Sorry. It's easier than it sounds.

Language Poetry   A movement officially beginning in the 70s, although influenced by the earlier works of poets such as Ezra Pound, Gertrude Stein, John Ashbery, and others. Language poetry attempts to subvert conventional narrative in order to create new possibilities for "meaning." Phrases may appear disjointed and incongruous, with more attention to the shapes of the letters than the words themselves, but the result is intended not as non-meaning but as a new exploration of meaning-making and of laying bare the processes of communication. There is an implication of social critique in this overhaul, aligned with Post-Structuralism in general. Some examples of language poets are Charles Bernstein, Susan Howe, Ron Silliman, and Lyn Hejinian.

John Cage   American Experimental/Minimalist composer (1912–1992). Using the principle of "indeterminacy," Cage allowed chance and accident to play the central role in his compositions. He experimented with atonality and electronics, as well as what he referred to as a "prepared piano," an instrument rigged with screws, bolts, cloth, rubber bands, and assorted small objects to replace the sounds of hammers hitting strings. He is most famous for 4′33″, a precisely timed piece composed for piano, in which no notes are played for the 4⅓-minute duration.

When you've filled the whole piece of swizzle with bumpkin strips, lay another strip of swizzle (sticky side down) across it, sealing all the ends. Trim to the doorway width using your trusty scissors. You can grommet some holes in the swizzle, use a hole-punch, or just staple it up to the doorframe. The bumpkin will glint and shimmer in the light, especially if you have a breeze, and it feels silky smooth when you walk through it.

Was that a little clearer? Maybe not, but I think it might be some kind of new art form.

LATEX RUBBER CURTAINS

Latex is the greatest stuff in the world, and you can make all kinds of things out of latex sheets, from clothing to room dividers, tablecloths, drapes, or rubbery cushion covers. I learned how to use this stuff from the design team at Eyefull, Inc., when I used to build sets for music videos, and we created amazing futuristic, stretchy, podlike environments with this technique. For the home, we mostly don't incorporate stretchy, podlike structures into our decor, but instead curtains are particularly beautiful as the latex has a glowy, translucent quality that's soft and luminous when light shines through. There's something very **Louise Bourgeois** about having all this rubbery stuff in your domicile.

Louise Bourgeois
French sculptor and installation artist (b. 1911). Having used all manner of materials during her long career, ranging from marble to wax to rubber, Bourgeois has created some of the creepiest and most disturbingly beautiful explorations of childhood and sexuality and the intersection of the two.

YOU'LL NEED

A bucket of clear liquid latex rubber (from a craft store or
    model-making supplier)
A sheet of plastic (clean, old shower curtain or drop cloth)
Roller with extension pole
Any latex paint
Paint tray and tray liner
Plastic bag
Baby powder
Grommets and shower curtain rings

Find a flat, empty space to lay out your plastic. Using an ordinary paint tray with liner and roller, roll out a coat of liquid latex directly onto the plastic and leave it to dry for a couple of hours. Wrap your roller tightly in a plastic bag between coats for the duration of the project and ditto for the tray or they will dry out and get all gunky and unusable before you've finished your piece.

If you'd like to add some spatters of color to the latex sheets, you can sprinkle any acrylic or latex paint onto the wet rubber. White looks super-cool for this. Make sure your paint is of a drippy consistency and not so thick that it falls in big gobs. If you do this between each coating of clear latex, you'll get a really unusual textural effect.

When the rubber coating and/or paint are dry, take off your shoes so you can walk on the sheet if you need to, and roll on a second layer of liquid latex. Lightly spatter the paint again if you are adding color. Keep on in this way until you've built up about five layers. When the latex is completely dry, sprinkle the whole surface with a thin coating of baby powder to prevent it from sticking to itself. Then, peel up a section of the sheet and fold it over to powder the exposed back of it. It may be difficult to get the edge started as it will be feathered to different thicknesses: just roll the latex edge toward the center with your fingers until it thickens enough to grab and peel up. Continue peeling, powdering as you peel so the sheet doesn't get bunched up and stuck together.

> **Vivian Westwood**
> English fashion designer (b. 1941) who, along with the notorious music producer Malcolm McLaren, created the original punk-rock style with her clothing designs incorporating zippers and rubber and S&M paraphernalia for 1970s London bands like the

Hold the sheet up to the light and notice how beautiful it is. Latex always sticks to latex, so you can glue dry pieces to each other by brushing on some of the wet stuff from the container. This way you can make things out of it if you're not satisfied with your beautifully translucent and stretchy curtain. You can also paint the latex onto surfaces like mesh or bubble wrap, and then peel it off for an interesting reverse-image texture. Liquid latex will destroy your clothes as it will dry into the fabric—though you can create interesting "rubberized" fabrics and clothing (think **Vivian Westwood**) by brushing latex evenly onto a lightweight, absorbent cloth. It will peel off your skin when it dries, though if some gets caught in a hairy place it can hurt when you pull it off. Some people are allergic to latex; if you are, you probably know already, since lots of things are made out of it, from rubber gloves to condoms, and in that case you should not do this project.

You can grommet these sheets and hang them with shower curtain rings from a rod. I'll bet you could make some really special upholstered outdoor furniture, too, though I never tried. Latex is waterproof, you see, so it is full of possibilities.

Wearables

Clothing, jewelry—it's all "**body art**" of one kind or another, whether you take it to the extreme of **Vito Acconci,** dressing up his penis in doll's clothes, or just dressing the rest of yourself up to go out for the evening. Dressing is fun and one of life's pleasures, and playing around with what you wear and how you wear it, and even making some of your wearables yourself, is all good.

Personalizing your clothing is one way of bringing art with you wherever you go. Of course, even completely ordinary clothing can figure as a work of art: check out **Charles Ray**'s *All My Clothes* (1973), which is a series of Polaroids of Ray

Vito Acconci American performance and video artist (b. 1940). His "seminal" work, *Seedbed* (1971), featured him masturbating under the gallery floor and pretty much indicates the limit of Acconci's willingness to explore and expose private space publicly. His interest in "power fields" informed *Seedbed* and other pieces, in which he hid in a public space to test an audience's ability to sense his presence.

Body Art The tradition of using the body as artistic medium, often overlapping with performance art. The pieces created usually involve actions either performed or recorded. Noted practitioners include Vito Acconci, Chris Burden, Carolee Schneeman, Yoko Ono, and Janine Antoni.

Charles Ray American contemporary sculptor (b. 1953). Ray has used his focus on self-portraiture and on humor as a means to explore themes of perception and identity via wide-ranging media. Projects include a life-size toy fire truck and a group sculpture of a dozen or so fiberglass Charles Rays all having an orgy with himself.

dressed up in various configurations of the items contained in his wardrobe.

The old cliché about Starving Artists is that they sit around in black turtlenecks and berets. Maybe that was true a few decades back, but it's not common in today's quickly evolving and ironically self-conscious culture. Starving Artists today are often recognizable by vibrant colors and patterns and one-of-a-kind thrift-store or homemade clothing items. You'll often see a geek-chic quality to a Starving Artist's style, complete with heavy glasses and clunky shoes, as smart equals sexy among most Starving Artists. Some Starving Artists sport the raga-muffin style, and they can pull off conflicting or odd patterns that others might not dare to try. When you see a gal in a pair of pants originally meant to be worn by somebody's grandfather, or a guy wearing his grandmother's former overcoat and shades, chances are they are Starving Artists.

A special note about bags: Bags are the number one greatest accessory of all time. This is because they can be outrageously funky, as many people will dare with a bag what they wouldn't on clothes and that's perfectly OK. It's probably because they are once removed from the actual person, being easily detachable. Anyway, pushing personal boundaries is a good thing. Just as long as you remember to fully explore your own bag personality. Bag-onality. Or whatever.

Felting Old into New

My *Webster's Dictionary* defines *felt* as "a cloth made of wool...through the action of heat, moisture, chemicals and pressure." Does this refer to a complex scientific process involving specialized equipment and toxic ingredients? Bah humbug! Felt is easy to make, especially the Starving Artist's way.

There exists an easy-to-use, easy-to-access machine for felt-making right at our fingertips, which by its very nature engages the actions of "heat, moisture, chemicals and pressure." That machine would be the ordinary household washing machine. If you put wool in a washer and turn it on (thereby adding a little "heat" and "moisture"), add some laundry detergent ("chemicals"), and let it do its centrifugal thing ("pressure"), you will end up with felt. Especially if you put the wool in the dryer afterward. The fibers will mat, shrink, and lock together and you'll get the dense, soft fabric commonly known as "felt." Voilà.

YOU'LL NEED

An old wool sweater

A washing machine, a dryer, and some detergent

Now, here comes the genius part: stop by your local thrift store and buy up any old sweaters made of wool. Run them through a hot wash cycle and a dryer, and the sweaters will get dramatically smaller and turn into felt. Once the sweaters have felted, you'll be able to cut the felt into squares. Unlike knitting, the felting process tightens the fibers in such a way that they will not unravel when cut. Note that some sweaters may need a second cycle to fully felt through: you be the judge.

All you need is two squares of the same size to make a cute felt pillow or bag. Cut out a flower or butterfly shape of a different color and stitch it onto the bag for the utmost in 60s Pop groovyness. If you have the architectural bug and a whole lot of time and ambition, you could make a groovy felt **yurt** like **Bucky Fuller** would do. Whatever you make, just throw your leftover scraps in the corner and it will feel like you have an original **Robert Morris** in your home.

Yurt A Mongolian circular domed tent, used by nomads. Yurts are constructed of a collapsible lattice frame and foldable felt walls. Useful if you move around a lot.

Robert Morris American conceptual and environmental artist (b. 1939). Morris has had a broad-ranging career that includes examining the effects of "gravity and stress" on heaps of felt, as well as creating blindfolded drawings and various projects examining the relationship between observer and observed and other contemporary ideas.

R. Buckminster "Bucky" Fuller American architect and philosopher (1895–1983) and inventor of the Geodesic Dome, Synergetics, and the World Game. As famous for his failures and far-out schemes as for his achievements, Bucky also wrote several books, including the amazingly titled *Operating Manual for Spaceship Earth.* Not to be confused with L. Ron Hubbard, the father of Scientology.

Avant-Garde A French phrase (from the Old French for "vanguard," which means those who lead an advancing army). Implies membership in an innovative group of the impossibly hip, usually artists, of course.

If you want to be totally arty, you can try making indefinable items by combining scraps of felt with fat or honey for the ultimate in **avant-garde** wacksterism à la **Joseph Beuys.** Or make an entire felt suit like he did—it's easy if you agree with the following quote from a 1970 interview by this granddaddy of German contemporary art: "Felt doesn't strive to be smart, so to speak. One has to conserve the character, omit mere trifles, such as complicated buttons, button-holes and so on, and if somebody wants to wear the suit, he can fasten it with safety pins." How convenient.

Joseph Beuys German artist (1921–1986). Part performer, part sculptor, Beuys focused on process and provocation using felt and fat and live wolves and a whole lot of other unusual stuff. He stated that art must be a vehicle for change and must be universal, not just a bunch of beautiful objects. Beuys is easy to recognize as he was often seen wearing a sort of fedora. FYI: the name is pronounced *"boys,"* in case you ever need to speak it aloud.

OLD SWEATER SLIPPERS

Once you've made some old sweater felt, the projects you can try are, in fact, endless. You can make a nurturing winged chair like **Gaetano Pesce,** since numbered among felt's greatest attributes are that it is soft

Gaetano Pesce Italian architect/designer (b. 1939) who perceived danger in uniformity, creating intentional imperfections in his works. His philosophy is to design with "ordinary" materials that are accessible without requiring major technology for production.

and soothing, comfortable and comforting. One of my personal favorite ideas is making felt slippers, and I've created a pattern for a cozy and *Hobbit*-y-looking pair that's easy to stitch up and you can pad around feeling like a transplant from Middle Earth. My friend Jeremy once told me that he thinks slippers are the single most important quality-of-life enhancer that he knows of. He's also extremely fond of grapefruits.

For the soles of these groovy slippers, you can use a thicker, sturdier felt from a heavy-knit sweater, though it doesn't have to be pretty since you're just walking on it. The uppers are nicest when made from lambswool, angora, or something else super-soft and luxurious—your slippers shouldn't feel like clunky, big,

Philip Guston American painter (1913–1980) who began his career as a Socialist Realist, moved toward Ab Ex, and ended up with a signature style of cartoony, semi-abstract painting characterized by his penchant for rendering lots of oversize, hobnailed boots.

Philip Guston booties, you want to relax and mellow out in them.

YOU'LL NEED

About 3–4 square feet of felt (approximately 1 sweater)
Some thread
Scissors and paper for copying the pattern

This pattern was designed to fit my foot (women's size 8), but I reduced it to fit it in the book. Photocopy the pattern on page 160 and blow up (did somebody say *Blow-*

Michelangelo Antonioni Italian Neo-Realist filmmaker (b. 1912) and director of the 1966 *Blow-Up*, a thriller and portrait of swinging 1960s London based on a Julio Cortázar short story, as well as *Zabriskie Point* (1970), which contains the surreal Death Valley love scene accompanied by Jerry Garcia's guitar improvisation. Director Brian DePalma remade the basic plot of *Blow-Up* with a small twist in his 1981 *Blow Out*, starring John Travolta.

Up? Is **Antonioni** in the house?) accordingly for your size difference. Just keep increasing until the size of the pattern creates a sole that is the right size to go under your foot. Incidentally, office jobs are helpful for all sorts of copying shenanigans, and I'd like to go on the record as grateful for the unintentional support of the various crummy companies that provided me stints as a Kafka-esque peon. If you are a Starving Artist and can't afford copies, go get a temp job! Cut out one set of the three pieces, then flip over the pattern and cut out the other foot. Stitch together according to the diagrams below. Feel free to embellish.

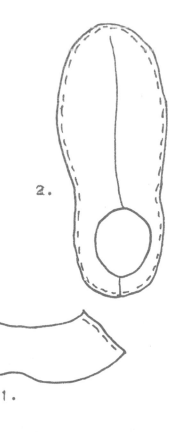

2.

1.

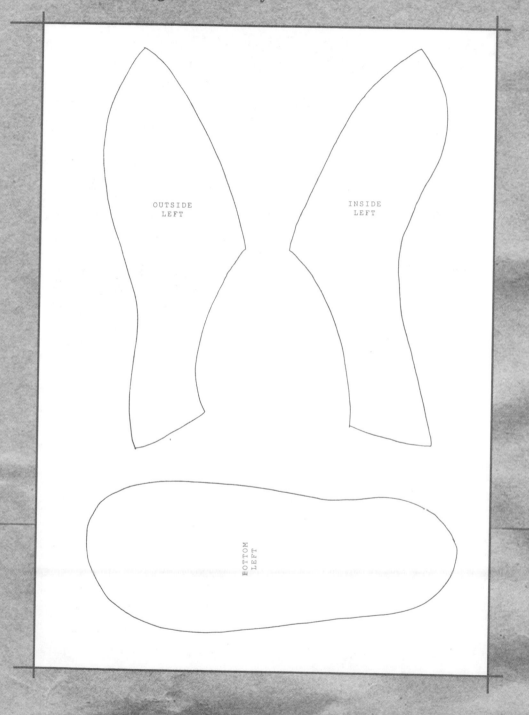

NO-KNIT HATS

Here is another good "Old Sweater Felt" project for anyone who's ever wanted to make a wool hat, but doesn't know how to knit or crochet. Your day has come. This one flies together in a jiffy, and you can choose any colors or decorations, which is the fun part, anyway. Play like you're **Helen Mirra** or **Arturo Herrera** while you're putting it together.

Helen Mirra
American installation artist (b. 1970) who frequently uses textiles, particularly felt, in her work.

Arturo Herrera Venezuelan-born contemporary artist (b. 1959) who uses cartoonish imagery combined with drippy abstraction and has created felt cut-out pieces that, though implying this same comical figuration, are actually just suggestive shapes and lines.

YOU'LL NEED
About a sweater's worth of felt
Needle, thread, and scissors

I've made two different patterns depending on what hat type you like. There's one with a brim, and there's your basic cone (nice with triangles of alternate colors and a tassel or pom-pom on the top). You can make a simple hat and dress it up with a little court-jester-y collection of felt scraps and strips. Very cute. Blow up the pattern of your choice on a copy machine until the sides will go comfortably around your head (about 2 times the size in this book). Cut out all the pattern pieces and sew together. Then flip inside out to hide the seams—or leave them showing for a trendy, reversed effect. The options here are endless.

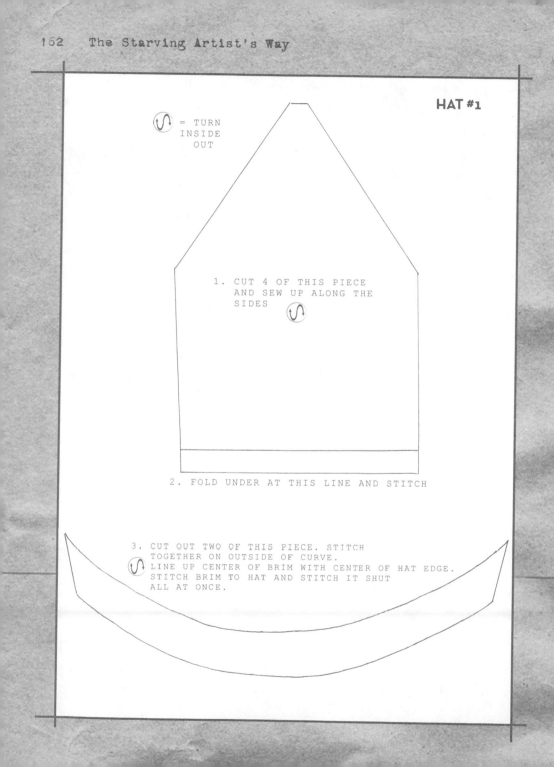

HAT #1

= TURN
INSIDE
OUT

1. CUT 4 OF THIS PIECE
   AND SEW UP ALONG THE
   SIDES

2. FOLD UNDER AT THIS LINE AND STITCH

3. CUT OUT TWO OF THIS PIECE. STITCH
   TOGETHER ON OUTSIDE OF CURVE.
   LINE UP CENTER OF BRIM WITH CENTER OF HAT EDGE.
   STITCH BRIM TO HAT AND STITCH IT SHUT
   ALL AT ONCE.

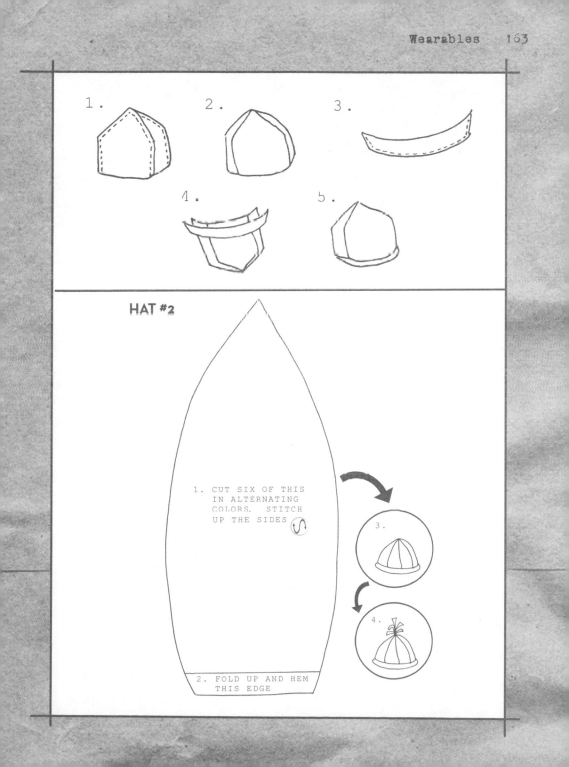

1.

2.

3.

4.

5.

HAT #2

1. CUT SIX OF THIS
   IN ALTERNATING
   COLORS. STITCH
   UP THE SIDES

3.

4.

2. FOLD UP AND HEM
   THIS EDGE

RE-WORKING MOTH-EATEN SWEATERS

No matter how careful I am, I always end up with a chewed-up sweater or two after the warm-weather, hide-away-your-wool season has ended. Even worse, the holes always seem to be right on the front, in the most horrifically visible spot as if the evil little Mothras had planned it that way. Now you could just decide to scrap your moth-eaten sweater in this situation, unraveling it to make something new, or shred it into **Hannah Wilke**-type feminist sculptures like lint vaginas. Or you can do one of the felt projects in this book. But let's say the sweater really fits and you'd like to hang on to it. Then just do a little fashion sweater-patch repair.

Hannah Wilke
American conceptual artist (1940–1993) interested in gender issues and the exploration of female sexuality. She used a wide range of media and was particularly fond of creating vaginal forms such as the gummies in the *Needed-Erase-Her Series* and the *Starification Object Series*.

YOU'LL NEED
Some felt scraps
Needle and thread

Step one is to stop the sweater from unraveling where the weave's been chewed by moths. This requires stitching around the hole like it's a buttonhole in order to bind the wool edges. Step two is to find a piece of wool felt and cut it into an appealing and flat shape for stitching over the opening. You could make an assortment of butterfly or "moth" silhouettes, some over holes, and some just randomly placed

Vladimir Nabokov Russian-born novelist (1899–1977) most famous for the controversial novel *Lolita* (1955), the story of European intellectual Humbert Humbert's unquenchable desire for a brash American schoolgirl. *Lolita* is considered by many to be, in fact, the story of a nonnative intellectual writer's fascination with the brash English language. The popular book was made into a horrific movie in the 1990s, but check out Stanley Kubrick's 1962 effort co-starring funny man Peter Sellers, aptly cast to capture the humor and absurdity of the provocative plot.

for a patterned effect. This would be a fitting and poetic tribute to the beast that devoured these holes in the first place, and is also a sly nod to the Russian author-cum-sometime-lepidopterist **Vladimir Nabokov,** which is an opportunity for intellectual props not to be missed. The butterflies can vary in size and are easily recognizable just from their outlines. **Damien Hirst** also did a butterfly series, so this image on your chest could associate you with his brand of bravado, and everyone will forget to smirk about the fact that you have holes in your sweater and instead stand back for fear that you may pickle an entire sheep before their very eyes.

Damien Hirst English conceptual artist (b. 1965). The best known of the Young British Artists (YBAs), Hirst was catapulted to prominence by the art collector Charles Saatchi, whose collection was the source of the controversial *Sensation* show at the Brooklyn Museum of Art in 1999. Hirst has pickled a variety of animals in his work as well as working with more traditional materials—like paint, which he spins in a self-designed contraption to create a type of centrifugal painting.

DOG HAIR / CAT HAIR FELT

I f you are in a position to harvest large amounts of dog or cat hair (i.e., you have some kind of furry animal in your house, leaving it all over the place), you can use the hair to make felt. I'm told you can spin the longer dog hairs into yarn, and there are books available on the subject, but I have cats, so I stick to felting, which can work with the shortish hair of cats.

Felting is definitely easier with longer hair, so if you have some wool fibers to combine with the pet hair, feel free. I was successful at felting pure cat hair, however, so I know it can be done. I'll be honest and tell you that felting from scratch is kind of labor-intensive, so unless you already know that you love it, I wouldn't count on completing any particularly massive felt projects out of pet hair. Maybe a small bag would be realistic.

Collect the hair from brushings until you have about enough to fill a shoebox. You don't need to wash it, as the felting process will wash it for you—just make sure there are no bits of lint or paper or other stuff mixed in with the hair.

YOU'LL NEED

Shoebox full of pet hair

Board large enough for your felt piece

Piece of canvas or muslin 2 times the length of desired felt piece

Rubber gloves

Dish soap

Hot water

Patience and a taste for the weird

Set up for felting by placing a piece of plywood or a cutting board in your sink. Lay a piece of canvas or muslin, which is twice the length of your proposed felt piece, on the board. Lay out the hairs in one layer and then lay out a layer of fibers perpendicular to these. Build up the hair until you have four or five layers. Cover the hair with the other half of the canvas.

Wear rubber gloves and sprinkle very hot soapy water onto the canvas. Press down with your hands to compact the fibers. Repeat this till the fibers feel really flat. Continue to sprinkle on hot water and, pressing firmly, make small circular movements with your hand on the surface of your canvas. Keep adding hot water and enough soap to make it easy to rub your hands on the surface without sticking. Turn your felt at right angles every minute or two.

Take a peek at your hairs at some point to see if they are matting together. If you can gently pull away the canvas and the hairs stay connected in a piece, you can take the top off your canvas and con-

tinue working it with hot water and rubbing the matted hairs directly. Eventually, you'll want to flip the felt and peel the canvas away entirely. Continue working with hot water until the piece shrinks and starts to feel "felted." When the felt is thick enough and strong enough for your purpose, you can rinse the remaining soap from it and spread it to dry on the wooden board. This whole project can take anywhere from about 20 minutes to 1 hour.

When you have enough felt, you can make a cat (or dog) change purse by cutting two pieces and stitching them together. Embroider or glue a face onto the surface. Fetishizing your beloved pet is a time-honored tradition, and you should feel good about this—ask **Carolee Schneemann** or **William Wegman,** both of whom have turned pet-o-philia into an art form.

Carolee Schneemann
American performance/body artist (b. 1939) best known for *Meat Joy* (1964), an orgiastic celebration with raw fish and other meats, and the fact that she unrolled a scroll from her vagina as part of an exploration of gender and the body. She has created numerous video projects with the collaboration of her cat, and her *Infinity Kisses* consists of eight years of documentation of mouth-to-mouth contact with the pet.

William Wegman American photographer (b. 1942) whose ubiquitous photos of an extended family of Weimaraners (descended from his first dogs, artfully known as Man Ray and Fay Ray) have made his name. The dogs are dressed up in various costumes and generally appear to be staring woefully at the camera.

CHAPTER TEN

Wardrobe Additions

Like a pioneer of the old frontier, the Starving Artist makes every attempt to stretch a dollar. In the Old West this meant darning socks and turning shirts inside out to reuse the side not yet bleached by the sun. Of course, the Starving Artist doesn't usually muck around to the same degree as those home-steaders because these days time is money. But a well-placed and hip decal can artfully and quickly cover a bleach stain in the spirit of our forefathers and provide the Starving Artist with a creative new T-shirt.

This chapter is meant to give ideas on how to supplement and en-hance your togs and to encourage you to think before you throw away. Any bit of cool fabric or trim can cover a ragged hem. A lone glove can be put to use any number of fun ways. Unrecognizable hardware store items can become rings and bracelets. You can turn something lame into something awesome in a matter of moments. Contained here are just a few ideas to get you started in realizing your own quirky fashion sense. Remember, if you make it yourself and you save money, too— that is cool.

BULL'S-EYE PATCH

One of the slickest ideas for covering up a hole or stain on any shirt is the bull's-eye patch, a decorative, direct, and daring reaction that beats the stain at its own game. It wouldn't be right for a true Starving Artist to slink off like a coward and allow a favorite piece of clothing to be destroyed through one moment of carelessness. Don't be afraid to take a stand; you never saw the ever-confident Pablo buckle to the rules of convention. Starving Artists do as they please, and a random accident may be a challenge, but not an ending.

> **Kenneth Noland** American Color Field/Op Art painter (b. 1924). It would be unfair and obviously an exaggeration to say that Kenneth Noland never painted anything but bull's-eyes. On the other hand, if you referred to "the bull's-eye painter," while a segment of the art world might think you were talking about Jasper Johns (see below) because he is more famous, much of the population, upon reflection, would figure out that you probably meant Noland.

This also happens to be the easiest cover-up patch ever: the **Kenneth Noland–Jasper Johns**–inspired bull's-eye cover-up patch.

> **Jasper Johns** American Neo-Expressionist/Pop Art painter (b. 1930). With thick, roughly applied paint, bright colors, and a nondimensional flatness, Johns created large-scale, reconceived versions of such recognizable symbols as bull's-eye targets, numbers, maps, and the American flag and dollar bill.

YOU'LL NEED

Scraps of felt or other fabric in 2 colors
Some circular things to trace (see below)
Scissors
Fabric glue
Thread (optional)

Here's how: pick two colors of a fabric that won't fray (felt is really nice for this and you already know how to make it), let's say blue and yellow, and draw out three circles of three different diameters, 1 inch, 2 inch, and 3 inch (if you trace around a quarter you will have the 1-inch diameter, the raised lip on an aluminum soda can is 2 inches, and the inside of a roll of packing tape has a diameter of almost 3 inches). Use one color for the 2-inch circle and the other for both the 1-inch and the 3-inch so the colors alternate.

Stack the circles in size order, making sure you center them, and using fabric glue, fix them to each other flat around the edges (smallest on top, of course) so you have a bull's-eye. Glue the bull's-eye over the stain or hole. Another option is to get some iron-on fabric from a sewing / crafts store and create the patch using that. You can stitch a circle of sloppy thread around the edge, once your patch is secure with glue, to make it look devil-may-care and roughly attached. You can also make more of these than you need and put them in a few places on an article of clothing to create a pattern, even if there's nothing to cover up. Who's telling you not to? You're the one making the rules here.

DRIP DOT SILK SCARVES

You can make a glamorous Hepburn-esque (any Hepburn will do) silk scarf from any salvaged piece of silk, from an old nightgown or shirt or a piece bought as a remnant. While it may seem retro and kind of "hanging with Cary Grant on the French Riviera," the silk neck scarf is actually a kind of **"futuristic"** accessory: notice how on a windy day the ends of fabric come swirling off your body in an **Umberto Boccioni** moment of unmatchable flair.

Futurism An artistic movement (led by poet Filippo Tommaso Marinetti), beginning in 1909–10, that started with a series of manifestos rejecting history and glorifying the machine. In the age of energy shortages and global warming it seems, ironically, a little old-fashioned.

Umberto Boccioni Italian Futurist painter/sculptor (1882–1916) who combined Cubist ideas with the fetishization of movement and is best known for the Futurist classic *Unique Forms of Continuity in Space* (1913).

YOU'LL NEED

A piece of silk approximately 20 inches square and a fairly light color, such as a pastel or off-white
Colored permanent inks or acrylic paint
Ink dropper or turkey baster

You can update a boring, inexpensive thrift-store scarf with this great Starving Artist method. Or, if you're starting from scratch with an ordinary piece of fabric, you should fold the edges over twice and make a tiny hem, sewing as close to the edge as you can, all the way around.

The colors can be applied to the silk with inks, paints, or dyes. Some inks will wash out, so do a test by applying a drop of the ink you have to a scrap of fabric and letting it sit and dry for 10 minutes. Place the fabric in a bowl of cold water for a moment to test if the stain will remain at all. Acrylic paint, thinned to the light consistency of ink, will work well, too. Use what you have and pick a few colors that will look great together. Whatever you use, mix your shades deep, as the final color will be lighter.

Polly Apfelbaum American installation artist (b. 1955) whose "fallen paintings" generally consist of bits of velvet stained by dye droplets and laid out in clustering shapes on the surface of the floor.

Once you have your dyeing medium chosen and ready, lay out your scarf on some newspaper. Using the dropper, pick up the first color, and from about 2 or 3 inches away, drop single droplets of color at intervals onto your scarf as if you are **Polly Apfelbaum.** Rinse the dropper. Decide if you want the colors to bleed into each other or to be distinct circles. If the latter, you need to wait for the first color to completely dry, or dry it with a hairdryer, before continuing. Apply the second color, and then the third. Keep in mind that you can do this with colors that are very similar, such as several shades of green or blue, if you want your scarf to be more subtle. You can definitely allow some of the drops to overlap slightly.

Leave the scarf to dry without moving it, so the color has a chance to really stain the fabric. It can sit for quite a long time if you have other things to do. When completely dry, rinse the scarf gently in a bowl of cold water to remove excess pigment. Some of the color will wash away, but it will leave lightened circular shapes of color. Spread to dry and lightly iron the silk, if necessary.

Wear with the panache of **Isadora Duncan,** but avoid falling prey to the sort of carelessness that tripped her up in the end.

> **Isadora Duncan** American dancer/choreographer (1877–1927). Known for her own personalized free-form modern dance and her radical politics (which led her to the former Soviet Union, where she met and briefly married the beloved Russian suicidal poet Sergei Esenin). Duncan is arguably most famous for the tragic absurdity of her own death by strangulation when her signature long scarf got caught in the moving wheel of her convertible.

LOST GLOVE ROOSTER / ANTLER HAT

This is a good way to put a lone glove to work, or even a mismatched pair. This project creates goofy fun out of a boring winter hat and is light-hearted during the dreary, cold season, when we all need some silliness to make us feel better. There may be some adults who aren't gutsy enough to wear this hat, though **Matthew Barney** would surely brave it (as would **Björk,** probably—maybe that's what they like about each other), but if nothing else it's a wacky headpiece for kids who are too little to object.

> **Matthew Barney** American video artist and filmmaker (b. 1967) best known for his *Cremaster* series of five films named and created out of numerical order. Barney appears in his own work in various incarnations, costumed most notably as a satyr, Harry Houdini, and Gary Gilmore, and surrounded by fantastical and dramatic imagery like girls swimming underwater, the destruction of expensive vintage cars, and Ursula Andress.

Björk Icelandic pop/electronica musician (b. 1965) and singer for the 1980s band the Sugarcubes, who embarked on a highly successful solo career in the early 90s. Theatrical, arty, and quirky in music and persona, she also starred in Lars von Trier's tragic movie musical, *Dancer in the Dark* (2000).

YOU'LL NEED

Wool hat
Old glove or two
A few handfuls of cotton wool or yarn scraps
Needle and thread

First, darn any holes in the glove, so the stuffing won't fall out, and then fill the glove with cotton wool or leftover yarn. You don't need to cram the glove full until it gets really round, just make sure you stuff a bit of filler down into each finger and the palm too, so it holds its general shape. Be sure to avoid letting it get too heavy, though.

Whether you will make a rooster hat or an antler hat depends on whether you have one glove or two. If you have only one, it's the rooster for you, and you should stitch the glove with the thumb facing forward right on top of the front of your hat. If two gloves, mount them opposite each other on the sides of your hat and above your ears. They will topple over, which is part of the intended look. You can stitch the hands to the hat along the side, down to the tip of the thumb, for greater stability. Getting yourself up in oddball costumes is a time-honored tradition worthy of extroverted artist types everywhere.

FOLDABLE SUN HAT

When constructed out of sturdy paper, this makes a good beach hat, which you don't have to worry about losing, as you can always make another. It's also good for parties, as the shape kind of gives the "wearing a lampshade" impression that every party needs as the night wears on.

YOU'LL NEED
Sturdy, decorative paper or oaktag
Scissors or matte knife
Duct tape

CUT SIX OF THIS PIECE
& FASTEN THE EDGES
TOGETHER

Blow up the pattern on a copy machine until the height of the bell-shaped outline is about 10 or 11 inches. Trace the pattern six times onto oaktag or heavy paper. Cut out the sides with scissors or a matte knife, depending on which is easier for you. Put 2 of the sides together, and using a 1-inch-wide strip of duct tape, tape down one side. Add the next piece and tape its edge to one of the free edges. Continue in this way until all the sides are taped together.

The last seam may be difficult to tape, as the hat won't flatten out so easily, but just be patient and you'll get it. Open the hat and try it on. The hat should be a nice deep bell shape. You can use a hole-punch to tie on strings over each ear if you're afraid of the hat blowing away.

Use an old umbrella to make a rain version of the same hat. Cut the six sides out of umbrella nylon. You can stitch the edges with fine thread and a small needle or tape with duct tape for a floppy, water-proof, and pocketable protector.

MAGRITTE SILKSCREENED T-SHIRTS

Lots of artists have used the silkscreen technique. Andy Warhol is (as always) the most famous, but there was also a slew of others, many of whom are mentioned elsewhere in this book. Silkscreens can be made from photos, but that requires money, chemicals, and either some know-how or the services of a trained professional. The Starving Artist's Way is cheaper and do-it-yourself, but you have to cut your own stencil, so it's best to keep it simple. Here's the scoop:

YOU'LL NEED

Piece of sheer fabric or old sheer curtain
A stretcher or old wooden picture frame
Paper and scissors
Staple gun and staples
X-Acto knife
Spray adhesive
Vinyl stick-on letters
T-shirt

Silkscreens are made of lightweight material that will allow ink or paint through, with certain areas masked off to create the image. An old sheer curtain from the thrift store is the perfect fabric for this task and will cost you next to nothing. You will also need an empty wooden stretcher or old frame, at least a few inches bigger than the image you choose to silkscreen, over which you will stretch a piece of the curtain, stapling it around the edges so it lies smooth and taut. Any painter is an expert in how to do this: start at the center of one side of the frame and staple the fabric. Gently pull across and staple directly opposite. Pull smooth to one of the perpendicular ends and staple the middle of that side. Pull across and staple the opposite middle. You now have a staple in the center of each side. Working from the center toward the corners, continue stapling the edges, smoothing the fabric taut before each staple and keeping out the wrinkles. It's just like preparing a canvas.

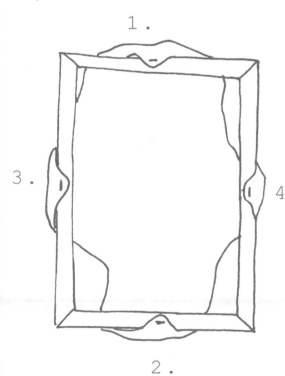

1.

2.

3.

4.

Now you have your screen. For the image to be silkscreened, you can blow up one of my silhouettes on page 180 to a size you like, or make your own by drawing or tracing an image onto paper. Cut out the design with an X-Acto knife, leaving the inverse of your image intact—this will be your stencil. Trim the outer edge of your paper so it will fit smoothly in the inside opening of your screen and using spray adhesive stick it in place. Press all the edges of your image firmly to the fabric so paint can't leak underneath. Use vinyl stick-on letters and spell out a word inside your image wherever it will fit. For my **Magritte**-inspired concept the key is to pick a word that has no apparent connection with the image—try any of the words below with any of the images. This randomness will provide that delightful touch of the surreal and is universally good for making things appear "arty."

Put a piece of stiff cardboard inside your shirt, so the paint won't bleed through to the back and so you can keep the shirt's surface smooth for an accurate transfer. Lay your screen onto the shirt, with the stencil drawing facing up and holding it still with one hand, brush some acrylic paint into the cut-out area of the stencil, making sure to fill the opening entirely and press down so the paint works through the lightweight fabric. When finished, lift the screen in one movement and check out your image. Wipe the back of the fabric screen clean of paint with a sponge if you plan to reuse your stencil, as the paint will clog the image as it dries. Make dozens more of these shirts and give them away—ease of duplication is the greatest attribute of the silkscreen.

René Magritte

Belgian Surrealist (1898–1967) who played with confounding the meaning of images and preventing ordinary associations. The distinguishing characteristics of a Magritte painting include lots of moody grayness, the recurring image of the bowler hat, texts that bear no relation to the objects they caption, and a subtle indefinable something that manages always to set your teeth on edge.

If you are gifted a shirt with an image on it that you hate you can just screen a big red "X" over the top and wear as usual. Or for a really simple project, you can cut out a basic shape, like a rectangle, and just put text in the center. You can make it joke-y, as **Richard Prince** would. If you've stained a shirt and want to use the silkscreen as a cover-up, rather than painting over

Richard Prince American photographer and Neo-Expressionist painter (b. 1949) who became famous in the 1980s for rephotographing existing advertising and Americana imagery, particularly Marlboro cowboys, copyrights be damned. He subsequently morphed into a painter of canvases containing mostly the painted texts of punch lines from bad jokes.

the mark, you might try stenciling a big, bright arrow pointing right at it instead. This is amusingly ironic and thus, very contemporary.

SPOON

TRUCK

TELEPHONE

PATCH POCKET/POCKET FOR A DAY

The whole raggedy-chic look makes some things a lot easier for the Starving Artist. Big, sloppy stitches can be inspiring—a sort of exploration of form and function, so you don't need to worry about perfection and you don't need access to a machine to stitch up hip-looking accessories.

In true ragamuffin **Alberto Burri** style, you can make this pocket-for-a-day and loose-stitch it to what you happen to be wearing: shirt, skirt, whatever.

Alberto Burri Italian Ab Ex painter (1915–1995) and former Italian army doctor who took up painting while a POW in Texas, during World War II. He painted on burlap and created collages out of rough scraps of the fabric combined with tar. He also created a series of "burned" pieces, referring to his technique as "combustione."

YOU'LL NEED
Piece of fabric the size of a pocket
Your chosen item of clothing
Needle and thread

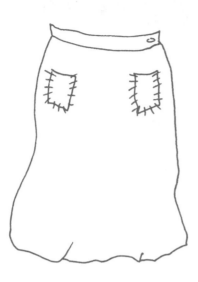

Just take a piece of fabric the size of the pocket you want (something sturdy that won't stretch too much, like flannel, cotton, or corduroy). Using good strong thread, sew the patch onto your clothing in a convenient and outrageous spot, leaving the top edge open for putting things inside. I predict this idea for temporary pockets will become the height of fashion any day now. It will become a new art form, referred to as "pocketing" and practiced by people from all walks of life. Don't wait and see—be one of the first on the block to take part in this exploration of the shifting nature of the experience we call "life."

DOUBLE BRAID BELT

At some point, every belt reaches its end. The holes rip out from overuse and you can fix them for only so long. Say goodbye, *sayonara,* or whatever, to the deteriorating, impermanent substance of which your belt is made. Not to the buckle, though. Oh no, never to the buckle; that would be silly. Buckles are made of metal or hard plastic and generally last far longer than the strip of pliable stuff meant to go around your waist. Cut the buckle out of the belt before you toss it and make a new belt out of it.

You can cut belts from strips of new leather, of course. But then you have to puncture neat holes that won't rip out and attach it to the belt with either a couple of rivets or some strong thread and a sturdy leather needle. Or you can avoid all that exhausting effort and make your belt the crafty way with rag braids, using leftover fabric and some **Rosie Lee Tompkins** resourceful, recycling stitchery.

YOU'LL NEED
Belt buckle
Colorful rags
Needle and thread

Choose fabrics that look good together, and rip nine 1-inch-wide strips of approximately two times your waist measurement. Rip straight lines by beginning the cut with a scissors and then ripping down the length of the fabric. Pull off any long, loose threads, but don't worry too much about the frayed edges—that's part of the look. Group the strips into sets of three and put a couple of stitches through the ends with a needle and thread to hold them together. Braid your three sets of fabric to the ends. Put a few stitches into each end to hold the braids, as well.

Loop each braid onto the buckle, one on either side of the tongue (the thin shaft of metal that goes in the hole) and one right over it, and stitch them securely in back. Sew along the lengths of the braids, stitching them together, to the end. Make sure the ends are securely sewn together and wrap the belt around your waist like you are **Jin Soo Kim,** with her trademark technique of wrapping all kinds of things in bandages. Attach your belt by poking the tongue through any convenient point in the braid.

> **Jin Soo Kim** Korean-born American installation artist and sculptor (b. 1950) whose works consist of metallic refuse transformed by being bandaged in gauze and other materials.

COIN NECKLACE

Jewelry can be made out of anything, but metal is always the longest lasting and thus the most serious looking and impressive. And now that the advent of the € (that's "Euro" to those of you who don't get out much) has swept away any use for the *centimes* or the *pesetas* that you may have kept stashed in a jar somewhere, you can put any leftover coinage to work with this idea for coin necklaces and bracelets. If you are now worrying that you've missed your chance for collecting glamorous, defunct European currency, don't despair. They still have beautifully ornamented coins in Mexico and all over the world that will work great for coin jewelry. Try getting them from a traveling

David Wojnarowicz
American multimedia artist and writer (1954–1992) who created brightly colored Pop Art paintings, and wrote memoirs and essays, both funny and poignant, on subjects like *Being Queer in America.* He lived in New York's East Village and died of AIDS in 1992.

friend, or take your own trip abroad with the pennies saved by being a thrifty, Starving Artist. You could certainly use U.S. coins as well, but I think it's considered illegal to mutilate them. It's also money, for God's sake, and extremely useful for buying things, not to mention graced with the images of dead presidents instead of the beautiful snakes, goddesses, and other great imagery you can find on many non-U.S. coins. But if you dare, flaunt the Federal Reserve and you can join the long line of artists who've used legal tender as imagery in their work, including **David Wojnarowicz.**

YOU'LL NEED
Several old coins
Jump rings and a clasp (or wire)
Drill and small bit for metal

Using a tiny drill bit, make two holes in each coin. Put the holes close to the edge and at about 2 o'clock and 10 o'clock when the coin is facing upright. You may miss with some of the holes and get too close to the edge, so have a few extra coins just in case you mangle some.

From a craft or bead store, buy a packet of those little C-shaped rings called "jump rings" to loop the coins together. You can use wire for this if you are extremely cheap or can't find jewelry supplies, but you will need to make sure the wire is sturdy enough to hold its shape without falling open, and then bend little snippets of it into closed loops. When you have enough coins to go around your neck (probably about 15 or 16, depending on the denomination) or wrist (maybe 7 or 8), put a jewelry clasp onto the ends so you can fasten it in place. How hot is that?

Coins tend to be bigger when they are worth more (the American dime vs. nickel relationship notwithstanding), so if you can get some big valuable ones, they will make for an extra decadent and dramatic-looking piece of jewelry. However, I'm not sure about the legality of wearing the coins in their country of origin. It's possible that you could find yourself in some kind of trouble for showing lack of proper respect for the king or queen of wherever it is that those coins come from. Although, if you do happen to get chucked in jail, don't despair; you could look at it as another artistic maneuver. Proceed with caution when traveling, which is always good advice anyway.

BALL BEARING NECKLACE

Ball bearings are some of the most amazing hardware store items. They look so damn good and they are a great invention to boot. In **Marguerite Duras**'s out-of-print novel *The Sailor from Gibraltar*, the ball-bearings king figures as an extraordinarily rich man, which is not hard to believe, given the many applications of

Marguerite Duras Vietnamese-born French author and filmmaker (1914–1996) whose best-known novel *The Lover* (1984) was made into a film directed by Jean-Jacques Annaud. She was the recipient in 1969 of the first pie-in-the-face thrown by the Belgian "comical terrorist" group led by Noel Godin, who considered her the epitome of the "empty" artist. Godin achieved worldwide fame in 1998 when his gang "pie'd" Bill Gates on a visit to Microsoft Belgium.

ball bearings. A necklace of ball bearings is a beautiful thing, a tribute to twentieth-century French women authors, and they can be easily wired together or looped with large jump rings and a clasp. Try the "fancy" option below as a great way to use a broken chain—just cut it into pieces with wire cutters.

> YOU'LL NEED
>
> *Several ball bearings*
>
> *Large jump rings and a clasp*
>
> *Five 1 1/2-inch segments of chain (optional)*

Ball bearings are open in the middle, so by using large enough jump rings you can just connect one to the next for a simple necklace or bracelet. If you want to get fancy, you can connect a ball bearing with jump rings or wire to a short piece of chain and attach the other end of the chain to another ball bearing. The final chain ends can be clasped together.

FOUND OBJECT CHARM BRACELET

In the 1950s all the girls had charm bracelets. They also had bobby socks and poodle skirts if movies like *Rebel without a Cause* can be trusted, and they had rock and roll, a handful of black-and-white TVs, and a few other memorable things. The cold war with Russia was in full swing back then, the McCarthy hearings were decimating the talent pool of the Hollywood Screenwriter's Guild, and in the art world the postwar movement in American painting had developed into what was to be known as Ab...but wait, I'm getting carried away. Charm bracelets. Right. Charm bracelets are back, and here's a way to customize yours in the DIY, Starving Artist's Way—practically for free. Let's get to it.

YOU'LL NEED

A 6-inch piece of chain
Several items for charms (see suggestions below)
Wire

First, for the bracelet: I like to use light steel chain from the hardware store. It's sturdy and can be cut to size by the clerks or at home with a handy pair of bolt cutters. Put a jewelry clasp on the ends of the chain to fasten the bracelet, or make it big enough to fit over your hand and join it by hooking the last two links and hammering shut. A bit of thin wire can also join the ends. It's so easy; really.

Now for the charms: Some funky things to use as charms are marbles, jacks, dice, single earrings, small bells, stones, beads, acorns, trinkets, tiny keys, Monopoly pieces—just about anything that is miniature and made of a virtually indestructible substance like metal, hard plastic, wood or stone. Or use the discarded exoskeletons formed of calcareous deposits, which minute sea creatures have formerly used to protect their soft and fragile corporeal beings (i.e., seashells).

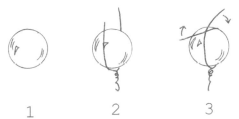

1   2   3   4   5

Use wire to attach the charms to the bracelet. Anything that doesn't have a hole in it needs to be caged with some thin wire (see the illustrations above). This is like wrapping a present with a bow. Wrap around once and then cross the wires and turn 90 degrees, wrapping around again to the top, and twist the ends together. Loop into a link of the bracelet, twist the ends together, and crimp. This is good for stones—you'll feel the influence of **Andy Goldsworthy** if you play around with nature's own art without altering it too much—as well as other solid objects like dice and marbles.

Andy Goldsworthy British environmental sculptor (b. 1956) whose temporary arrangements in nature of leaves, rocks, snow, and other natural, found materials are photographed to preserve the moment of visual order he imposes.

Wear your super-cool charm bracelet with the pride of someone who has constructed a mini **Rauschenberg assemblage.** OK, so this project doesn't have anything as startling as a bed or a stuffed eagle in it, but Rauschenberg's giant fabrications couldn't be worn on your wrist. So we're even.

> **Robert Rauschenberg** American Pop Art painter and assemblage artist (b. 1925). Originally an Ab Ex painter, Rauschenberg developed a signature sculptural style of brushing drippy paint onto all manner of found objects—even an eagle and a goat—and mounting the whole thing on a canvas. He also worked with newsprint transfer, silkscreen, and commercial imagery and is considered one of the original Pop artists, helping to define the genre.

> **Assemblage** Term coined in the 1950s by artist Jean Dubuffet, referring to 3D collage and inevitably including the use of all kinds of nonart objects such as taxidermed animals, dishes, furniture, and eventually anything imaginable. Robert Rauschenberg, Louise Nevelson, Louise Bourgeois, Joseph Beuys, and Joseph Cornell all famously experimented with this sort of conglomerative work.

Marble Pendants

To make a pendant, you can use the above technique for putting a beautiful old marble or any small object you love onto a chain. The chain can be a lamp cord or anything else you like, and the object can be caged in wire, as described above, and looped onto the chain. Wearing something unusual always intrigues people, and being intriguing and unusual on a budget is the Starving Artist's Way.

HOT GLUE JEWELRY

Hot glue is an incredibly versatile material, which can be used for all sorts of purposes and effects, from just attaching small objects together, to making the cobwebby, intricate strands for Hot Glue Lace (see page 142) or the rubbery pools for this project.

Artist **Tom Friedman** makes hot glue gems by placing droplets of the glue onto magazine pages. When the glue hardens, Friedman pulls it up and the image is attached to the back of the drop. These have appeared in his work as fantastical water beads. Running with that idea, you can also make small "pools" of hot glue for larger jewels than those Friedman creates. These are great for rings or pendants, even magnets (see page 81), though keep in mind that the image will be partly obscured by the cloudiness of the glue—bright colors of no particular pattern are your best choices, and the slightly faded quality gives a retro cast to the imagery. You can decorate an entire tabletop with hot glue jewels. They can be glued to a surface or you can make small holes in them with a needle or pushpin and string them together with jump rings for a necklace or earrings.

You can use hot glue as a less toxic, though less translucent, resin alternative. When you find a beautiful dead ladybug or bumblebee lying on the ground or the windowsill, don't think: "Uck! Dead bug!" Think: "Scarab." Think: "Amber with preserved insect." Think: "Artifact." Think: "**Ed Kienholz** would probably dig this." You can make your own mummified bug jewelry that will keep forever in the following way:

Tom Friedman Contemporary American artist (b. 1965) who uses everyday materials, transforming them with intensive labor and imagination into elaborate and often humorous works of art. His most famous pieces include a self-portrait carved onto an aspirin and a sculpture formed from an endless strand of spaghetti.

YOU'LL NEED

A bottle cap
An insect or other artifact
Hot glue and glue gun
Hammer and nail
chain

Find a bottle cap that you like, and that is big enough to house your found insect. Rinse it out, and if it's misshapen, use a pair of pliers to bend the edges back into shape. Glue in a colored background if you want to or just lay your insect into the bottom. Now you need a hardening agent in which to preserve the bug: just let the hot glue flow. You'll

Ed Kienholz American installation / assemblage artist (1927–1994) who, along with wife Nancy Kienholz (b. 1944), made often grotesque room-size diorama installations full of thrift-store items as diverse as furniture, car parts, skeletons, a Coke machine, and horse hooves. When collected the result is a kind of retro nightmare scenario. They also made Joseph Cornell (see page 111)–type smaller assemblage boxes with equally oddball contents.

want to cover the bug completely, but not overflow the bottle cap. The glue will be cloudier than resin, and probably contain some small air bubbles, but that makes the whole thing look mysterious. Hot glue dries in a few seconds. When the glue is dry, use a hammer and a nail to drive a small hole through the raised rim of the bottle cap. Put the cap on a chain or lamp cord and wear around your neck for an ancient artifact pendant.

You can also put a small photograph in a bottle cap and seal over with poly or glue for a special locket.

CHAPTER ELEVEN

Bags

RETRO EASY KNIT BAGS

If you've ever wanted to knit something, but all you know is straight knit and nothing about increasing, decreasing, cabling, or the like, join the club. I can knit, but I don't know how to follow complex patterns to make those strange shapes you need for sweaters and the rest, and I don't have the time or motivation to learn, either. As it turns out, I can make a great knit bag anyway, and pretend I am **Rosemarie Trockel** while I am doing it. This retro bag looks awesome and nobody can believe how easy it is. It's a fantastic basic knitting project for anybody who only makes scarves and doesn't need another one.

Rosemarie Trockel
German conceptual artist (b. 1952) whose most famous series involves using computers to create "knitted" paintings. The images are usually repetitions of logos and pop culture artifacts, and their crafted and patterned re-creation explores the nexus of art and labor, technology, and "women's work."

YOU'LL NEED
knitting needles (I like fat ones)
A couple of skeins of sturdy, thick yarn
Needle and thread

I recommend using a double thickness of yarn for extra strength. It also looks dynamic if you use two different colors knitted together.

First, determine the width of your bag. I usually cast on 36 of my double-thickness stitches in heavy wool onto fat needles, so I am able to fit a folder or notebook into my finished bag. It will take knitting only one line of stitches to figure out if that's not going to be wide enough for you, so just experiment at first with the number of stitches until you're satisfied. Then, knit about 60 to 100 rows of stitches or until the piece is a little more than twice the depth you want for your bag. Good, done with that part.

For the strap, cast on 7 or 8 stitches—this will be the width of the strap, so adapt accordingly if you want it narrower or wider and then knit about 100 rows. The strap is going to stretch if you ever put anything heavy in the bag, so it's okay to be a little bit conservative on the length (if the strap ultimately stretches too much, rather than scrap the bag you can detach the strap, rip out enough lines of knitting to make it the right length, and then reattach it).

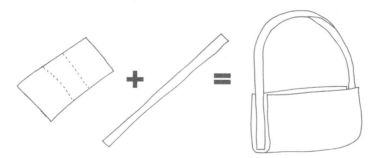

Lastly, with a strand of yarn and a fat needle, sew the strap onto the main piece. The strap ends should form the sides of the bag (see illustration) and then the strap loop extends upward. Stitch together the seams around each end of the strap, and make sure these connections are strong—sew it all twice if you need to.

For added sturdiness, and if you are using wool yarn, you can stir the bag in boiling water for about 20 minutes on top of the stove. This will cause the surface to fuzzy-up a bit (i.e., "boiled wool"), but the yarns will also lock to each other and become more strongly fastened than when just knit. You won't get this effect with synthetic yarns, so don't bother. Be prepared for the color to fade slightly if you boil it, but this adds to the cool, retro attitude you are going for with a bag like this. If you are using more than one color of yarn, the colors will blend a bit as the dyes bleed out and color each other, so consider that as well when choosing yarn hues.

You can make the same basic bag out of fabric if you can't or won't knit, by cutting one piece to be the strap and sides—say, 3 inches wide by 5 feet long and the other for the main body at maybe 30 inches long by 16 inches wide. Just stitch the 2 pieces together on the wrong side and then flip right-side out.

A couple of pockets on the outside are also useful for any bag, and double pockets on the same side are particularly trendy. Make them 5 inches high by 4 inches wide and iron the edges under ½ inch before stitching flat to the bag.

BUTTON BASKET

Words fail me. This one's so much easier to do than to describe that I think it would be best to approach it as a comic strip. I'll include text so you can follow the "plot."

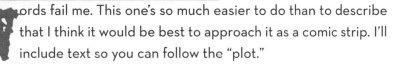

YOU'LL NEED
A bunch of buttons (224 to be exact)
Wire and wire cutters

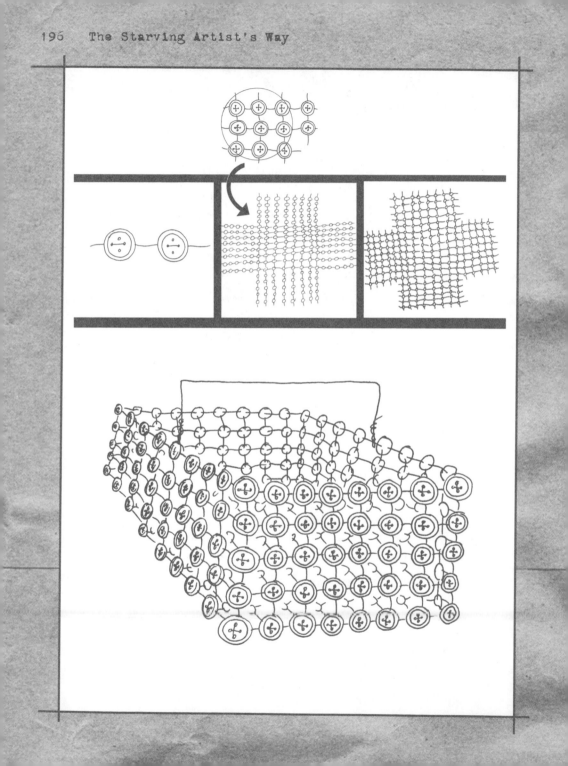

1. Use only buttons that have four holes. And also be sure to use a light-gauge wire—if the wire's too thick, it will be hard to work with. String the buttons on the wire in long strips with each button about 1 inch apart. Since you are threading through 2 holes, the buttons will have no trouble staying put on the wire. String 18 buttons per wire on the diagonal, leaving 1 inch of wire at each end. Make 8 of these strands.

2. Lay out these strands side by side on a table. Start a new strand stringing on 5 buttons and then picking up one of the completed 18-button strands and weave across the sixth button in each piece, making a grid formation. After you have strung all 8 of the long pieces add 5 more buttons, each 1 inch apart. Make 8 of these new strands and all rows will be threaded. This will create a grid that is 8 buttons wide by 8 buttons high, with strands of 5 buttons each continuing off in all directions.

3. Thread across the rows on each side to create 4 panels jutting off the center.

4. Wire the panels to each other in a box formation. The sides will be 5 buttons high and the bottom will be 8 by 8.

5. Make a little wire handle across the top. Finito. A wire-and-button concave portable receptacle—aka "a basket."

You can also do this with bottle caps if you make 4 small holes in each with a drill or a hammer and nail. If you like buttons, though, stashes of them are easy to come by at yard sales and thrift stores. There are cheap plastic ones, fancy metal ones, and all kinds of other

Charles LeDray   American contemporary sculptor (b. 1960) who creates miniature objects out of a variety of unusual materials. He has carved a stalk of wheat and several buttons from human bone.

beauties. Maybe there'll even be one or two **Charles LeDray** buttons thrown into the mix. Shiver.

A related suggestion from artist/fashion designer Moi Tran for a project that can use up a big button collection: "beaded" curtains made from strands of threaded buttons. Use a curtain rod that fills a window or doorway. Thread the buttons, knotted in place every 2 inches, onto strings or strong threads that fill the length of the opening (i.e., floor to ceiling). Tie the strings to the curtain rod and let them hang. This idea is especially stylish if you use buttons of just one or two colors instead of total multicolor. Using all different red and orange buttons, for example, can look really spiffy and avoid the mishmash catch-all look of too much going on at once.

PLASTIC BAG BAG

Did I mention yet that *anything* can be made into a bag? No doubt I did. Well, how about the ultimate in re-conceiving form—making a bag out of bags. The idea itself is as poetic as poetry, and even **Frank O'Hara** would have to approve of the nitty-gritty nod to the profundity of plastic.

Frank O'Hara   American poet (1926-1966) who was an art lover and worked for years at the Museum of Modern Art in New York. His notable enjoyment of the lowbrow and his lack of interest in poetry as a mere reflection on nature is most evident in the famous lines from his 1954 poem "Meditations in an Emergency," "I can't even enjoy a blade of grass unless I know there's a subway handy, or a record store or some other sign that people do not totally regret life."

YOU'LL NEED

A heap of plastic grocery bags in the colors of your choice

A piece of plastic or canvas mesh (I use a plastic mesh from a craft store, which is meant for rug hooking—a **Judy Pfaff**-type metal mesh might work if it's bendable)

Something with a dull point (an unsharpened pencil, a knitting needle, the eye end of a large sewing needle)

Scissors

Judy Pfaff   American installation artist (b. 1946) who used a combination of painting and sculpture with swirling, squiggly, bright-colored, and plastic-y forms.

Decide on a pattern. As most of my grocery bags tend to be black or white, I like the checkerboard pattern. When finished it looks stripe-y like a zebra. Whatever you choose, you should keep it simple, as highly specific patterns usually don't read clearly in the end. You can always make the thing random or one-color if you don't want to get too elaborate.

Cut the plastic bags into strips. You can work out the most comfortable size, but I like them ½ inch wide by 3½ inches long. Just measure one and then make the rest of them look more or less the same.

Take the first strip, and using your dullish pointed implement, push the end of the strip into one of the mesh holes. If you poke too hard, you'll poke a hole right through your plastic bag—the idea is to nudge the strip through the mesh opening so that you can grab it on the other side and pull it most of the way through. Then poke the other end through the adjoining hole and pull so both ends are even. Tie a single knot as if you are about to tie your shoes and stop before the point where you'd make the bows. This will hold the piece in place and prevent you from tugging this strip out when you are trying to grab the next one.

Continue in this way, starting the next strip in the same hole where you finished the previous one until you've carpeted the mesh. For the checkerboard, do five of one color and then switch for five of the next color.

If a small rug or mat is what you want, then you can leave it like this. For the bag, just fold the rug in half, with the protruding ends on the outside, and stitch up the sides with strong thread through the mesh holes. Add a handle of braided plastic bag and attach to the mesh at either end of the opening.

DUCT TAPE WALLET

D uct tape is one of those amazingly versatile materials. With it you can accomplish just about any task. You can attach things to each other, make endless useful items, and even seal some ducts should the need arise. It's incredibly sturdy, but also fibrous and flexible and comes in several colors.

Sure, you can keep your money in one of those fancy leather wallets, but a wallet is the kind of possession that disappears all too easily—getting lost or stolen more often than you'd like. It's annoying having to replace all your credit cards and IDs, but if you have a wallet that you can replace with an outlay of only pennies at the hardware store, you'll cheer right up. Not to mention the slick 1980s industrial, post-punk vibe that duct tape gives off at all times. This one draws comments when-ever you whip it out in public. Further-more, you don't have to be **Frank Gehry** to figure out how to construct one of these things. It's all made out of tape, for Pete's sake.

Frank Gehry Canadian architect (b. 1929). One of the best known of all contemporary architects, Gehry is widely ap-preciated for his design of the Guggenheim Museum in Bilbao, Spain, a space for art complete with giant metallic sails, giving it the perfect look to be Gehry's representative "flagship."

YOU'LL NEED
Duct tape
Scissors
Measuring device

Lay out a 21-inch strip of duct tape sticky side up. Put down another next to it, with a slight overlap. Keep on laying strips side by side until you reach a 4-inch width. Then lay strips of tape facedown (sticky sides now facing each other) on top of these to create a 21 by 4-inch piece of duct tape "fabric." Every time you need a new piece of duct material, this is how you'll make it. Trim, if necessary, to the correct size.

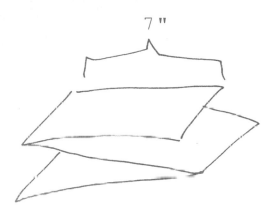

7 "

Make a mark 7 inches from each end and accordion-fold the piece to make a ∠ shape.

Leaving one side loose, tape the bottom and side of two of these segments together, making the pouch that will hold your bills. Fold the wallet in half at the middle point and press with your hands to make a crease here.

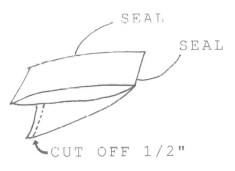

SEAL

SEAL

CUT OFF 1/2 "

Cut ½ inch off the loose end and then fold it two-thirds of the way toward the crease, then over again. Tape the bottom edge shut. Tape the top edge of the inner fold to the bill compartment, creating a small top pocket, as well as an inside pocket.

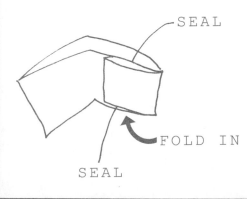

SEAL

FOLD IN

SEAL

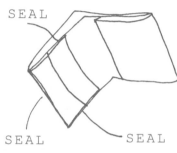

SEAL

SEAL   SEAL

Cut a piece of duct material 4 by 4½ inches and fold one-third over and tape sides to make shallow pocket. Tape this inside the wallet around the three outer edges, leaving two pockets facing the wallet's center. Be careful not to tape the bill compartment shut.

If you will need a change compartment (I personally cannot live without one), you can tape it onto the outside of the wallet. Cut a piece of duct fabric 7 by 4 inches and fold over 1 inch to make a flap 1 by 4 inches. Fold the remaining 6 inches in half to the crease. Tape the base of this pouch to the outer surface of the wallet and then tape the 3-inch sides shut on both edges. Take a small strip of stick-on Velcro (available at most hardware and 99-cent stores) and place one bit under the 1-inch

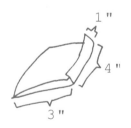

1 "

4 "

3 "

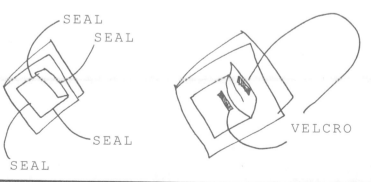

SEAL

SEAL

SEAL

SEAL

VELCRO

flap with its mate opposite. Tape around each piece with more duct tape, just overlapping slightly on every edge, so the Velcro can't pull off. Obviously, people require different elements in a wallet—it's a metaphor for natural difference: just as no two snowflakes are alike, so too no duct tape wallet is right for everyone. That said, you can feel free to adjust compartments for your wallet as you see fit. For example, tape in a panel of clear acetate if you need a place for an ID to show through.

FOUND OBJECT POCKET BAG

Any working artist, starving or otherwise, is familiar with the vinyl slide sheet. With ever more common digital formats, slides may soon become a thing of the past, but for decades the 35 millimeter slide has been the format of choice for archiving images of artwork, and the slide sleeve has been the format for archiving these slides. When the slide sleeves get too scuffed up, as can happen after they've been sent out for countless grant applications from which you were rejected, leaving you without the funds to buy new slide sleeves, it's time to retire them from professional duty. This is a good project for those dingy sheets. You can also find plastic sheets for business cards and photos, so you have your choice. Poke around the aisles at the stationery store.

YOU'LL NEED

A pair of clear slide sleeves (side-loading for a horizontal bag)

Fishing line and a needle

A length of chain

Take two slide sleeves and match them up with the pocket openings all facing up. Line them up back to back (I like the pockets on the outside) and stitch around three sides with fishing line, leaving the "top" open, which mirrors the pocket opening. Attach a handle on each end through the holes meant for binder rings, and use a pull chain or other lightweight chain from the hardware store, attached with a bit of twisty wire. You've got your bag. Put some spare pennies in a few of the pockets, maybe a ticket stub or other small item, and an odd earring or two. Maybe even a slide. Anything special, graphic or fun, will do. Put your usual things in the larger opening and enjoy the touch of exhibitionism that this bag encourages, as your possessions will be as naked as a model in a **Vanessa Beecroft** installation.

Vanessa Beecroft

Italian installation artist (b. 1969). The provocative Beecroft is difficult to categorize, as her work consists almost entirely of arranged groups of nude or semi-nude models, usually young women in wigs and high-heeled shoes, standing around until they tire and sit down. She has created similar pieces involving fully clothed formations of U.S. Navy SEALs—the human bodies becoming the medium for Beecroft's vision of "sculpture."

UMBRELLA DRAWSTRING BEACH BAG

If you walk around a pedestrians' city like New York on a rainy day, the most notable sign of the state of the weather, besides the droplets of water, the wet streets, and your frizzing hair, is the fact that on every corner garbage cans are stuffed with umbrellas that have malfunctioned and been sidelined by dissatisfied consumers. This is not a sparkly *Umbrellas of Cherbourg* scene by **Jacques Demy,** but the point is that even if you don't happen to possess the carcass of your own lame, ruined umbrella, you usually can find one for free on pretty much any city street-corner on a wet day.

Jacques Demy French New Wave filmmaker (1931–1990) who directed the visually outrageous, hyper-romantic, and completely unusual operatic musical *The Umbrellas of Cherbourg* (1964), starring the very young Catherine Deneuve. Notice the sneaky art direction in the scene where her dress is the same pattern as the wallpaper.

Christo Bulgarian-born environmental artist (b. 1935). The man who wraps things is known even outside of art circles. For several weeks at a time, Christo, in collaboration with wife Jeanne-Claude, envelops elements of landscape, from entire small islands to architectural structures like buildings, bridges, or say, Reichstags, in voluminous sheets. His *Umbrella Project* is uncharacteristically unwrapped and located in Japan and California.

What to do with these things? Well, you can, of course, create your very own massively scaled land work if you like. I don't want you to feel that your imagination is being limited by the scope of this book. **Christo** did a nifty *Umbrella Project* using, oh, thousands of umbrellas. That's not so hard. Or you could surely manage a homage to Walter de Maria's *Lightning Field* if you went up on a very tall place and raised your umbrella's metal frame as high as you can reach. But I already talked about Walter de Maria (see page 95) earlier in this book. So, let's do a safe and manageable project.

YOU'LL NEED
Fabric from a defunct umbrella
Grommets (or needle and thread)
Sturdy cord

Usually when an umbrella fails it's a problem with the spokes and hinges. For this project you'll ditch all of that. Carefully cut the threads that hold the fabric in place. At the umbrella's point, there's a cap that usually screws off to let the material loose and when you lay it out flat it becomes a rough circle. Now, there are several options. You can cut out the center and make an emergency poncho, or sew in a bit of elastic to craft a waterproof circle skirt. Or see the instructions in this book for a foldable sun hat (see page 176). Otherwise, you can make a lightweight and waterproof drawstring bag—perfect for carrying wet suits home after a day in the sun and surf at the beach. Using rain gear on sunny days is one way to try to pull the old switcheroo on the weather—a game that might comfort you for the fact that actually you have absolutely no control over the weather whatsoever. Useless but amusing acts of bravado in the face of powerlessness are in keeping with the Starving Artist's Way.

The instructions are simple: Grommet a hole about 2 inches down from each point on the umbrella's edge. You don't want to be too close to an edge or seam, or the fabric might rip out of the grommet. Then, put in another grommet about midway between these points,

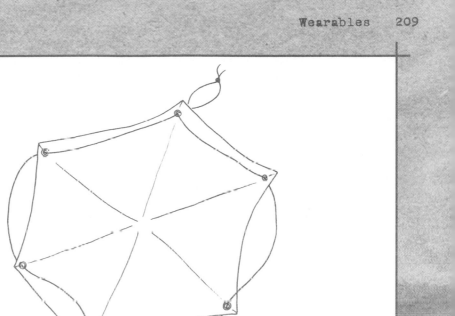

again a couple of inches from the edge. A note about grommets: they are inserted by use of an inexpensive and simple tool, but if you can't find one, you can sew small holes, button-hole style. The point is just to reinforce the hole so it doesn't simply start a rip that tears through to the edge of your fabric.

Take a 2-foot length of strong, smooth cord and thread it into one hole and out the next. When you have threaded through all the grommets, take your two ends and tie them to each other. When the strings hang loose the bag falls open automatically. When you pull on the string to pick it up, it pulls shut and you can sling the cord over a shoulder. This bag is kind of interactive that way. The umbrella bag is good for lightweight stuff—nothing too heavy. You can make the same bag with a circle of sturdier material if you need to carry weightier stuff. Don't be too demanding here—this one was recycled and basically free.

Potions

It's a no-brainer that you can waste a lot of money on cosmetics, and mostly they're all made out of water anyway. Try making your own when you can, and maybe buy only the one or two favorites that you can't live without. That is the Starving Artist's Way.

The tradition of using one's own body as a sort of canvas for exploring artistic ideas is a time-honored one that you can approach as deeply as you like. No need to take a bullet in the arm, like **Chris Burden,** or have yourself cut with razors, denuded, and almost shot in the head, like **Marina Abramovic.** Keep it skin deep.

Chris Burden
American conceptual performance artist (b. 1946) who was catapulted to fame with his piece *Shoot* (1971), in which he had himself shot in the arm. Burden's later works include gallery-size models of buildings, bridges, and other manly structures.

Marina Abramovic   Serbian performance/body artist (b. 1946) who was influenced by the Viennese Actionists. In *Rhythm* O (1974), she passively presented herself, along with a variety of "instruments," as available for viewers to manipulate. Among other things, she was slashed with razor blades until the performance was canceled when a loaded gun was placed to her head.

Cosmetics

"OPERATION MARGARINE" MOISTURIZER

What is a moisturizer anyway? Obviously it's something that keeps your skin from drying out. Can you slather plain old oil on your face and be done with it? Ugh, no. Even if that sounded fun, we all have a pretty good idea of the difference between greasy and moist. A moisturizer has oil in it, sure, but it also contains water, which is what you're trying to get your skin to drink up and keep in. The other essential ingredient in moisturizers is an emulsifier—that's the thing that keeps the oil and water blended. Moisturizers may also have some vitamin E and some vitamin A. Besides being good for your skin, those vitamins are also natural preservatives.

Have you ever thought about what is in a stick of margarine? Despite the **Roland Barthes** reference in the title, I'm not asking for ironic cultural criticism here, but rather the more literal answer: oil, water, and an emulsifier and some other weird stuff with long,

Roland Barthes French cultural and literary critic (1915–1980) who wrote about the distinction between meaning and language, about themes of mass culture, and the "connotations" of seemingly innocent things and ideas. In *Mythologies*, a collection of essays, he writes of *Operation Margarine*, a metaphor for society's fickle ability to accept the unacceptable.

suspicious names. I can't be responsible if you don't use an all-natural brand. A common emulsifier in margarine is lecithin, which occurs naturally in plants and animals. If you have lightly salted margarine, that's fine. There is salt all over your skin already and it can't hurt. If you use soy margarine, you'll have some protein in the mix, too, like those expensive collagen creams. Some margarine brands already contain vitamin A either in place of other preservatives or in the form of beta-carotene for coloring, which is the same thing that makes carrots orange. If your brand doesn't have vitamin A and you want to add it—no big deal! Just get some capsules at the health food store along with some vitamin E, and you have all the ingredients you'll need for an economical moisturizer.

Transforming a stick of margarine, an exceedingly evocative icon of 1950s low culture, into the supremely classy-sounding "protein and vitamin enriched moisturizer" smacks of **Andy Warhol** and his soup-cans-turned-high-art sensibility. This is a nice bonus as you'll feel very Pop Art every time you use it. Feel free to follow through on this idea by giving margarine moisturizer as a gift, with the original brand logo glued to the lid of the jar.

Andy Warhol American Pop artist (1928–1987). The most famous of Pop artists, Warhol was born in Pittsburgh and died in New York, after once surviving an attempt on his life. (See *I Shot Andy Warhol* for a cinematic depiction of this incident or *Basquiat*, since superstar David Bowie plays superstar Warhol in that movie.) Warhol started as a commercial illustrator who applied this sensibility to the world of fine art, along with such themes as cultural obsession with media, fame, consumerism, etc. Warhol is most famous for his painted Campbell's soup cans and for silkscreens of Marilyn Monroe and other celebrities. Warhol is also renowned for his "Factory," the one-time locus of downtown hipness, where artists and musicians (i.e., the Velvet Underground) gathered and experimented.

YOU'LL NEED

Margarine
Empty cosmetics container
Vitamins A and/or E, essential oil (optional)

I keep my margarine moisturizer in an empty plastic container with a screw-on lid that once held some other sort of cosmetic that I don't waste my money on anymore. If you don't have one of these you can use any small jar. All you've got to do is mash half a stick of margarine into your container. If you want to add vitamin E or A, prick several of the capsules with a pin, a pair of scissors, or your teeth and add the oil to the margarine. Toss away the empty capsule. Then, blend the whole business together with a spoon or your fingers until it feels pretty uniform.

If you're making a body moisturizer, feel free to add a drop or two of vanilla to the mix or any essential oil you might particularly like. Rosemary, lavender, and clove all have antiseptic properties (and smell good, too) if that is important to you. A few drops of avocado oil can go into the mixture if you need something extra rich and soothing.

This stuff is not hard science, so don't come calling if you know a few extra-credit facts about beta-carotene or lecithin that you think I didn't explain properly. I know what I need to know, which is that it works for me and keeps me looking eternally young. Actually, the greatest thing about this moisturizer is that not only is it good and cheap, but it is also thick and creamy, and smearing it on your body is almost as fun as eating it, but without all the calories! Just as you would when contemplating a **Tibetan butter sculpture,** remember to ponder the "impermanence of all things" when applying this stuff in front of a mirror.

Tibetan Butter Sculpture   Along with the sand mandala, it is one of the most important of ancient Tibetan Buddhist arts, symbolizing impermanence. Yak butter is mixed with pigment and groups of monks sculpt the stuff into brightly colored flowers and animals. The Tibetan New Year is the most common time for butter sculpture, when over the course of several hours or days extremely elaborate pieces are constructed, and then ritually destroyed.

"HAND" SOAP

Yes, you can make soap by inducing a chemical reaction of lye and fat. And it's a very good idea. I highly recommend it. However, I'm not going to get into how to do that, because you can get recipes all over the Web or out of books from the library without my help. You can also buy what's called "melt and pour" soap from craft stores and soap supply Web sites (just search for the term "melt and pour") if what you want is to scent the soaps and make shapes and you don't care about actually making your own. The true quick and dirty S.A. method for soap-making, though, is just to melt down existing bars of soap and reshape them. It's best not to add scents to these unless they are unscented, as the smell could get overpowering, but if you buy a couple of bars of fragrance-free soap you can then add a few drops of any essential oil to the melted mixture for home-designed smellification. You can add your own colorings, again keeping an eye on how existing soap color will affect the finished result. There are soap pigments available from the same folks who sell "melt and pour," or you can use food coloring, preferably oil-based, from a baking supply store. Or just buy a soap you know you already like and you can mold it into shapes for cheap gifts at holiday time.

YOU'LL NEED

Soap

Essential oil (optional)

Food coloring or soap-making pigment (optional)

Grater or food processor

Double boiler (or equivalent set up—see below)

Safety gear

Rubber gloves

Patience

To melt soap bars, chop them into 1-inch pieces and grate them in a food processor. Then put the grated bits in the top of a double boiler or a small pot set into a larger pot of boiling water on the stove. Burning soap smells nasty, so don't put the soap in a pot directly over the flame. You might want to add a spoonful per bar of additional oil, like olive or avocado, for their moisturizing properties. And you can stir in a spoonful of water if necessary so the soap mixture forms a paste. Then, stirring occasionally, let the soap melt until it's moldable. If it doesn't get smooth enough or if you want a fluffy "whipped soap," you can put the soap paste in a bowl and beat it with an electric mixer until smooth.

Finally, you can pour the melted soap into molds of your choosing. Or try any of the following super-easy ideas:

1. Take a rubber dishwashing glove and lightly rub the inside with a coat of Vaseline. Using a clothes pin, attach the end of the glove to a hook or a nail, so that it's firmly gripped and hanging with the fingers pointing down. Give it a tug to make sure it will stay put when weighted.

When the soap is ready, pour or spoon it into the rubber glove carefully to avoid spills and burns and allow it to fill the hand at least up to the wrist. Be careful with the hot soap. Wear gloves and goggles.

Allow the soap to cool and set. It will take several weeks for the soap to completely harden, so be patient. You can peel back the glove a bit at a time to check if the exposed portion feels solid. When ready to remove, carefully peel back the glove to remove the soap. It will, of course, be shaped like a hand. It will need some more drying time once it is exposed to the air and it will shrink a bit and get kind of creepy and shriveled.

Use as any other soap, but with additional thoughts of **Salvador Dalí** and **Surrealism** in general. If giving as a gift, wrap a ribbon around the wrist with the label "Hand Soap" lest there be any confusion about the fact that this is "hand soap."

> **Salvador Dalí** Spanish Surrealist painter (1904–1989) and colorful character who is most famous for his painting *The Persistence of Memory* (1931), picturing a bunch of clocks draped all over a landscape. Also known for his creation of the famous dream sequence in Hitchcock's classic movie *Spellbound* and for the artfully twirled, enormous off-the-hook mustache he sported.

> **Surrealism** An artistic outgrowth of Dada, the movement was led by the poet André Breton in the 1920s and focused on an interest in the unconscious, in dreams, and in the desire to unburden thought from the encumbrances of consciousness and morality.

2. Another type of quick soap is mold-free "imitation seashell soap," which is "hand soap" of another sort, your own hand being the mold. Don't add water to this one and only melt the soap mixture

slightly so it is a little bit mushy, but firm enough to hold a shape. Remove the soap from the heat and wait until it's cool enough to touch. Take a small handful and squeeze gently into a loose fist, just until some of the soap seeps between your fingers. Then put the "shell" on a sheet of waxed paper or plate to dry and make a few more. These should dry in about a day as they are exposed to air on all sides and have only minimal moisture in them.

3. Another easy soap project is to pour melted, smoothly whipped soap into a rectangular plastic salad bar container and let it dry for a day or two. Then, tip the soap cake out onto a sheet of waxed paper and use a cookie cutter to make shapes. Allow the pieces to dry completely. You can also emboss the soap pieces when they are almost dry with a carved item of metal or wood pressed firmly into its surface. Press into the soap with interesting jewelry or the handles of ornate silverware arranged in a "flower" formation. Or, try a hand-shaped cookie cutter—these are fairly common and can be bought from a good kitchenware supplier—for another version of "hand soap."

Free soap tip: For the most basic in recycling ideas, melt the little scraps of leftover bars that are too small to use anymore with just a touch of water and re-form into a newly usable bar.

OATMEAL AND ALMOND SCRUB

Whatever else you may do to stay clean and breathtakingly beautiful, you'll want to use an occasional bit of gentle grit rubbed over your face to remove the residue of dullifying, dry, dead skin. Think of it as a light buff with fine sandpaper before the final, perfect, glossy varnish topcoat. Or think of it as taking care of your skin properly. Whatever. But it's a good idea to exfoliate once or twice a week. Anyway, that's what all those Eastern European former beauty queens who give inexpensive facials in New York's East Village are always telling me.

YOU'LL NEED

1/2 cup raw almonds

1/2 cup raw rolled oats

Baking soda (optional)

Grind the almonds with the oats in a food processor. I like to mix in a tablespoon of baking soda as well, and this becomes my twice-weekly exfoliating scrub.

Oatmeal, almond meal, and baking soda are all mildly abrasive and provide good scrubbing action. At the same time, the oatmeal and almond are both soothing and moisturizing, and the baking soda disinfects and helps to remove blackheads.

Place about a tablespoon of the powder in your palm, and mix with warm water. *Gently* rub onto your face. Try doing those little circles with your fingertips like they do at a spa and give yourself a mood-enhancing face massage. Leave the mixture on for a minute or so, and take care of any business that takes a minute or so to take care of and then rinse it off. If you videotape yourself putting this scrub on and removing it, you can entertain yourself with thoughts that you are doing a **Bruce Nauman** piece—it might keep you from getting bored by the tedium of an extra cleansing routine. Even without the videotaped proof, you can enliven the exfoliation procedure by contemplating the idea that your new ritual is more than beautification, it's a bit of **"Actionism."**

Bruce Nauman American conceptual artist (b. 1941). Widely regarded as one of the most influential artists of the late twentieth century, Nauman has played with video, installation, drawings, tape recordings, neon, holograms, and anything else he likes in order to embody his explorations of language and communication, most of which are riddled with pun and jokiness in the service of his belief that all his activities are art.

Actionism Vienna-based art movement beginning in the late 1950s, and founded by a group of performance/body artists who used ritualistic action as a vehicle for art. As an outgrowth of Happenings and Fluxus (see page 264), Actionism explored the seamy underbelly of human psychology and myth, with projects at times so extreme that artist Rudolph Schwarzkogler, for example, killed himself in 1969 with a series of art shock treatments.

RETRO SHAVING SOAP

A touch of retro chic can transform penny-pinching into style. Notice the difference between the two words *used* and *vintage*. The perky *vintage* easily outclasses a dumb word like *used* and fetches twice the price on eBay. It's all about how you spin it, but at the end of the day *vintage* is just old with an attitude.

The shaving brush and cup of soap is an example of a cheaper, simpler alternative that can infuse your mundane morning hair removal with that groovy feeling of olden days, when down-and-out guys wore hats cocked at rakish, devil-may-care angles while they slouched on street corners and ate pie at midnight in moody **Edward Hopper** locales.

Edward Hopper American Realist painter (1882–1967) whose works are almost universally desolate, lonely, and moody. Among his paintings is the famous *Night Hawks* (1942), the incessantly reproduced depiction of the after-hours corner coffee shop.

YOU'LL NEED

Shaving brush

Mug or cup

A bar of soap

Double boiler (or equivalent arrangement)

Avocado or olive oil (optional)

Lavender essential oil for scenting (optional)

Experience the magic yourself or just give it as a gift. First, you'll need a shaving brush, which you can buy at many pharmacies or department stores. Old Spice makes a ceramic one for around $5 or $6. The cup can be purchased at a junk shop and should be of your own choosing, though I like the classic white diner coffee mug best for this project. These two props are your main investment. While you have to lay out some extra cash for them up front, the shaving soap you make will last for years and definitely save you money in the long run. As a gift it is an obvious bargain.

Melt a bar's worth of your favorite well-lathering soap (Dove is good for this purpose) by chopping it into squares and grating it into a double boiler. Add 1 tablespoon of avocado or olive oil for extra emollient skin soothing, while the soap is still soft enough to stir in. If your soap is unscented and you want to add a drop of lavender essential oil, you can do that now. Transfer the soap mixture to a bowl and beat until smooth with an electric mixer, whisk, or an extremely fast-moving fork. Pour or spoon the soap into the mug, and allow it to set for a few days until it hardens. When ready, wet your brush, lather up ferociously in the cup, and go to it. The aura of **Jacob Lawrence**'s *Barber Shop* will begin floating through your mornings once you've ditched the boring and badly packaged spray-on stuff for the nifty brush-on *retro* shaving soap. I hear shaving is way more fun this way.

> ## Jacob Lawrence
> American Dynamic Cubist painter (1917–2000). He painted with tempera and completed several series on the lives of important black figures and events, including *The Migration of the Negro to the North,* as well as scenes from daily life such as the above-mentioned barber shop. Lawrence taught at Black Mountain College with Josef Albers in the 1940s.

SALAD DRESSING SKIN CLEANSER

Here's a skin cleanser that will save you loads of cash in the drugstore cosmetics department, as well as being healthier than all of those chemical concoctions with a million ingredients. My musician sister Samara Lubelski suggested the first part of this cleansing procedure, and the second part is my own invention. We were each using our own homemade skin treatment with no notion that together we were making a salad dressing facial. Apparently my sister and I go together like oil and vinegar, which is to say both willingly and with a certain amount of resistance to blending smoothly. Sisters are like that, you know.

YOU'LL NEED
Oil and vinegar
Water
Cotton balls

Step 1: Samara recommends removing eye and face makeup with a cotton ball soaked in olive oil. You can use a clean cotton ball to wipe off any excess makeup or oil. This procedure doesn't dry out or irritate sensitive skin, but it gets all of the gunk off your face.

Step 2: I use a mixture of one part apple cider vinegar to five or six parts water as a postcleansing toner. I swear. Put some of the mixture on a clean cotton ball and using a circular motion, rub it gently over your whole face. The vinegar cleans off residual dirt and oil, as well as killing germs on the skin's surface and leaving a protective acidic coating. If the cotton ball looks dirty when you finish, repeat the procedure until you're fresh and clean enough to dare a **John Coplans** close-up.

I wish I could recommend following these steps with an application of lettuce leaf on your face, but I don't think it's necessarily beneficial to wear an entire salad every day. I do know, however, that many fruits and vegetables are helpful for different skin conditions, so lying down for 10 to 15 minutes with cucumber slices over your eyes and some mashed tomato or avocado on your skin to combat some or other unsightly imperfections might do you some good. Feel free to check out the full-on salad treatment if that sounds relaxing to you.

John Coplans   English-born photographer (b. 1920) who was the founding editor of *Artforum*. Coplans was a former abstract painter who took up photography at the age of 60. His work consists of large, oppressively close-up black-and-white photos of various parts of his own inarguably aging body.

Spectacular Special Events and Gifts

Making your gatherings and events memorable even if you don't have time for that in your normal life is an important aspect of "living it up," something that art is here to remind us how to do. A touch of decorative icing on the cake, a present in unusual wrapping, personalized gifts, and special foods are all the little bits that make up an artful and memorable occasion. Just think about **Martin Kippenberger**'s altruistic, artistic goal of "spreading a good mood." If you can achieve that, you will never go wrong.

And live it up with your mementos and the gifts you give, too. Wrap your presents so friends are inspired to fold and save the packaging. Make cards that family will hang on the wall long after the season is over. It doesn't have to cost a bundle and it doesn't have to take a year to prepare. Just give everybody a sparkle of something never seen before.

> **Martin Kippenberger**
> German painter and installation artist (1953–1997) considered particularly fun-loving when it comes to art. Among other amusing works, he began creation, before his death, of a global system of subway entrances, which lead inevitably to nowhere as the actual global subway system they imply is nonexistent.

CHAPTER THIRTEEN

Gift Wrapping

EASY / FUNKY WRAPPING IDEAS

Save on wrapping paper: start with plain butcher paper or Kraft paper and then add decorations.

1. Make Hot Glue Jewels (see page 191) and then glue them to wrapping paper or cards for a glistening Viennese-themed **Klimt** or **Hundertwasser** effect.

Gustav Klimt Austrian Art Nouveau painter (1862-1918) who led the Vienna Secession, a break-away movement by the Austrian avant-garde. His most popular paintings show human figures surrounded by flat, decorative costumes of gold with touches of painted mosaic, and his *The Kiss* (1908) has become something of a staple among college dorm room reproduction posters.

Friedensreich Hundertwasser Austrian painter and architect (b. 1928) whose works are influenced by the Viennese Art Nouveau tradition and the designs of Antoni Gaudí, Art Nouveau architect. Full of vibrant color, decorative elements, humor, and humanist ideology, his oddball paintings include one that depicts rain falling on a car roof from the point of view of the rain droplets. His architectural projects involved the design of myriad houses with grass roofs, and also his advocating of the right of rental tenants to decorate the façades of their buildings as far as they can reach out of any window.

2. Glue 20 to 30 different all-one-color, flat plastic buttons onto the package.

3. Make a potato print like you did in kindergarten. Cut the raw potato in half and then make a raised image on its surface by carving away around it. You can create an image with a cookie cutter, bottle cap, or any metal object and then cut off the excess. Print with tempera or thinned acrylic paint onto your wrapping paper for a homemade pattern.

4. Use ribbons—these can be strips of any bright or shiny fabric. If you wrap the paper neatly, you can get away with frayed ribbon edges for the au naturel look and it will seem like you meant it to be that way.

5. Put a few stickers on the package, as that always keeps the excitement level high. Don't forget to save stickers from junk mail for this purpose—it doesn't really matter what they say. Also, you can buy those red dot stickers from the stationery store—they may mean "sold" in a gallery, but they mean "sold to someone who bought it especially for you" on a gift. Or print out images from the Internet onto label sheets and cut them out.

6. If you are personally lacking in the area of skilled penmanship you can try this classic idea for gift cards or even funky wedding invitations. Just like the covers of the Sex Pistols albums designed by **Jamie Reid,** you too can approximate the edgy ransom-note look that's become a staple of popular culture. The text should be cut from magazines or newspapers and glued onto cards with an eye to varying capitals and lowercase. Try to begin words with lower-

Jamie Reid English graphic artist (b.1947) who was a school friend of Malcolm McLaren, legendary manager of the Sex Pistols, and who was tapped by McLaren to be the art director for the band's posters and record sleeves. Reid was interested in the Situationists, an artistic group founded in 1957 that focused on political action, manifestos, and pointing out the absurdities of capitalism. His work for the band became a vehicle for him to explore the expression of political ideas. He's particularly remembered for popularizing the lo-fi, cut-out letter look.

case and include at least one capital in the body of the word without rigidly switching back and forth—the look of randomness is the key here. Intentional misspelling is always fun too, as in "happie burthday," "happee holliedays," and "congradyoolashuns."

7. Make "product placement" gift tags (see below). Cut logos and funny bits of packaging out of cartons. Cut out a window. Glue the cardboard onto white or light-colored paper. Hole-punch the end of the tag and write a holiday message in the window. Then tie it to a gift with a bit of cord or ribbon. This is a quick sort of greeting/labeling device that says "I love you enough to spare a tree's life in your name." Feel free to write this sentence on the back of the card if it suits your mood and if you have recycled the paper for your backing. Otherwise it's dishonest, though if you feel you can get away with it, far be it from me to intervene. True or not, the recipient will feel good if he or she is convinced of the truth of this statement. And feeling good all around is the goal of giving, after all.

8. Use Deco Paper Flowers or Citrus Netting Gift Bags as described below and on the next few pages.

DECO PAPER FLOWERS

Packaging is an essential part of gift giving. Spectacular wrappings can liven up even an uninspired gift, causing the lucky recipients to enjoy the unwrapping process so much that they don't even really register that they don't want or need the thing you gave them. They might not notice until they get home that the gift is actually small, previously owned, and/or distinctly inexpensive. So, particularly if you don't have a lot of money to spend, the extra time you take on the visual details of your packets will make people appreciate your well-meant but economical gifts anyway. But, of course, you should endeavor to give exceptionally nice gifts to your friends and family at all times. Anyway, here's an easy-to-create cut-out flower that inspires people to paroxysms of delight when they see the gift you've brought them. Made from five easy pieces:

> **Art Deco** A decorative style of the 1920s and 30s, which achieved great and lasting popularity and is most recognizable for bold outlining of shapes and rectilinear forms.

YOU'LL NEED

2 contrasting sheets of colored paper

Scissors (the most valuable tool I know; you don't hear a lot of odes or rhapsodies on the scissors subject, but I have a pair in every room of my apartment—I'm not sure what other item I could say that about)

Stapler

Choose two sheets of colored typing paper or construction paper in contrasting colors like blue and orange, pink and green, or black and

white. Using the templates above, cut sizes 1, 3, and 5 from one color and sizes 2 and 4 from the other.

Stack the pieces in size order, with the three smaller cut-outs positioned perpendicular to the larger ones.

Put two staples in the center, making an X and pinning the stack together.

You can fold each flower petal along its center line, which will give the flower some height.

Stick onto packages with a loop of Scotch tape underneath. Or you can staple these flowers onto pipe cleaners for an entire bouquet. They look kind of stylized jungly in the mood of the ultimate outsider artist **Henri Rousseau.**

Henri Rousseau   French Post-Impressionist painter (1844–1910) and retired customs officer. With no art training, Rousseau began painting in middle age and was more or less "discovered" by Picasso and his cronies. His paintings are dreamlike jungle scenes with wild beasts and large, decorative, and leafy undergrowth.

CITRUS NETTING GIFT BAGS

If you buy oranges by the dozen, or lemons or limes in almost any grouping greater than about three, you may find that they are packaged in net bags of various pleasing colors corresponding to the color of the fruit. Do not throw these away. These nets can be used for all kinds of things, the most obvious of which are great little gift bags. (For example, you could fill one with an entire family of Row-of-Ducks Candles [see page 241] or a half dozen small Imitation-Seashell Hand Soaps [see page 215]). Or the ambitious among you can even figure out a way to do an **Eva Hesse** sculpture. Or not.

Eva Hesse   German-born American Abstract sculptor (1936–1970) who used netting and tubing, cloth, and a host of other nontraditional materials, as well as metals and Minimalist sensibilities, in the service of organic themes.

YOU'LL NEED
Recycled piece of fruit netting
Small piece of a cardboard carton
Scissors
Stapler

The netting is generally a tube with a knot in one end and a label on the other. Cut down the bag to the size you need with scissors, and cut off the paper tag on the end. You can leave the knot as the bottom of the bag, or knot one end yourself if you've had to trim the bag down. Then fill the net bag with the chosen gift items or even just some boring old candy. Cut a piece of heavy paper or a bit of one of last year's holiday cards into a rectangle that is approximately 4 by 3 inches and fold in half to make it 2 by 3 inches. Catch the open ends of your bag between the cardboard ends and staple shut along the open edge of the card with an ordinary desk stapler. Decorate the cardboard as a gift tag with season's greetings, "from:" and "to:" labeling, explanations, or instructions for unusual contents or some stickers.

Cards

SEED PACKET NOTE CARDS

Meg Fry, dancer and choreographer, contributed this clever Pop Art card and gift idea. Meg buys several packets of seeds from the hardware store, which can be used over and over again for this project. The pictures on the packets can be of flowers or vegetables, but they always look great, and are just the right size.

YOU'LL NEED
Seed packet or other fun imagery
Card stock
Scissors and glue stick
Paper cutter
Some cash for the color copy machine

Cut a small sliver off the top, bottom, and right edge of the packet (you can save the seeds in something else, like an empty film canister), but leave the left edge intact so the packet opens like a folded card.

Tape or glue several of these packets flat onto a sheet of paper.

At a copy shop, make color copies onto white or light-colored card stock. If you use a colored paper, like beige or gray, the colors will be slightly altered but still really neat. You can choose glossy or matte.

Lay the images out to fit as many packets as possible on a single sheet of paper and then run off as many as you need of the page. Keep the original for future card sets. Cut out the cards and fold in half so the packet's back becomes the back of the card. (You can buy a paper cutter for less than $20 if you plan to make a lot of these, or use the paper cutter at the copy shop for cutting the sheets—it looks much smoother than if cut with scissors.)

If you want the cards to fit a standard envelope size you may need to enlarge or reduce your copies to get the size right. Or you can make your own envelopes with the instructions in this book.

You can also use favorite product images from various other types of packaging to make cards. Meg's done a series of cards of "old time girls" using Sun-Maid raisins and Morton's salt girls (sounds like **Henry Darger,** but without the Civil War weapons and eerie male genitalia). Just cut and lay the images out to make a great card design, and copy that.

If you get into making cards often, invest in having a rubber stamp custom-manufactured at create-a-stamp.com. Try one that says "Cards by So-and-So" to stamp on the backs of your creations. Or design a logo for yourself and have that made into a rubber stamp.

Henry Darger American illustrator (1892–1972). Darger was born and died in Chicago. He grew up in an institution for disabled children, eventually living alone as an adult and working as a janitor. When he wasn't working, Darger filled his small apartment with a monumental 15, 145-page illustrated novel peopled with armies of little girls involved in gory eviscerations and strangulations. He also made huge watercolor scenes, and a diary in which he recorded nothing but the weather for ten years. His collected works were discovered after his death and were kicked around for a while before ending up in the Museum of American Folk Art in New York City, making Darger into a big name in contemporary art and *the* name in contemporary outsider art.

You can write any message on the inside, or tie a ribbon around a set of a half dozen or more of these cards to give as a gift.

3-D POP-UP PICTURE CARDS

Pop-up cards really impress people when they're homemade because there's a slight element of engineering to them that appears difficult to achieve. People often assume that these cards are created with "technical know-how" that the layperson could not master. However, the structure is not difficult at all, being a question of the most basic math, as simple as a **Mel Bochner** diagram. Here's how.

> **Mel Bochner**
> American conceptual artist (b. 1940) whose 1960s "Measurement" series consisted of diagrams on gallery walls of the rooms that contained them.

YOU'LL NEED
Sheet of card stock
An image to pop up
Scissors and a ruler
Sheet of typing paper
Glue

You can use cut-outs from magazines for this project or use your own photos, drawings, or text. Glue your image to card stock or a piece of a cereal box so it is smoothly attached and sturdy. Cut a strip of paper that is 1 inch wide and the height of your image *times two, plus another 2 inches* (remember "times 2 plus 2"). See the pictures to clarify these instructions. For example, let's say your picture is of a killer bee and is 2 inches high. For this bee you would use a strip of paper that is

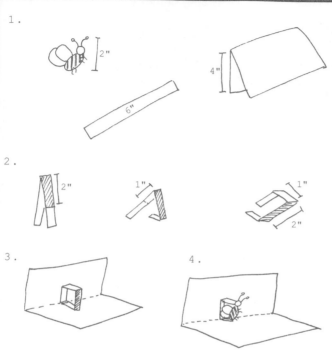

1.

2.

3.

4.

6 inches ($2 \times 2 + 2 = 6$). A 3-inch picture of a baby platypus would require a strip that is 8 inches ($3 \times 2 + 2 = 8$). Fold a card whose width is at least 2 inches more than your image's height. So, the 2-inch killer bee needs a card with a width of at least 4 inches. The baby platypus card would have a width of at least 5 inches. Fold the paper strip in half and then mark the height of the killer bee from this centerfold. Fold the paper strip inward at this point—it should be 1 inch from the end. Fold the other end of the strip at 1 inch from the center point. When seen sideways, the paper strip now makes a sort of rectangle, with a width of 1 inch and a length of your image size. Glue the open ends of the folded paper strip flat at the seam in the card.

Glue your killer bee onto the portion of the strip jutting up perpendicular to the right hand of the card. Fold forward to close the card. Open the card and see the killer bee pop upright. Aaaaah! Killer Bee! Get it? Scary as a **Paul McCarthy** video...

Paul McCarthy   American sculptor, video, and performance artist (b. 1945) whose works are goofy grotesqueries of childhood fairytales and fantasies. He's known for sex jokes and scatology and big messes of ketchup, as well as the newly commissioned giant cartoony inflatable sculptures outside the Tate Modern in London. His classic video, *Heidi*, made in collaboration with artist Mike Kelley, was followed by the much gorier tribute *Heidi 2*, artists Sue De Beer and Laura Parnes's 1999 "unauthorized sequel" showing the further horrific adventures of a much-abused rag doll.

HOMEMADE ENVELOPES WITH LICKABLE GLUE

Make your own envelopes for invitations or to go along with gift cards. Cut out the pattern below after blowing it up to fit your purpose. Fold in flaps A and B toward the center. Glue the edges of flap C onto the edges of flaps A and B. Fold to crease flap D. It's not a **Rem Koolhaas** blueprint, but I think the drawing will help.

If you are sending these off one time, you can just use a glue stick to seal them shut, but if you plan to give the envelopes as gifts or for RSVP cards, you should make some good-tasting and nontoxic lickable glue and paste it along the edge. Here's the recipe.

Rem Koolhaas   Dutch architect (b. 1944) and co-founder of the Office for Metropolitan Architecture. He is known for early conceptual projects like *The Berlin Wall as Architecture* (1970), which examined the impact of structures and of absences on the surrounding area. Also widely known for his book *Delirious New York: Retroactive Manifesto for Manhattan* (1978).

YOU'LL NEED

1 (1/4 oz) packet unflavored gelatin
1/4 cup boiling water
2 tablespoons sugar
1/2 teaspoon vanilla extract

Mix all ingredients. Make sure the gelatin and the sugar are dissolved and then allow the mixture to cool for a minute or two.

Brush a line of the mixture onto the envelope along the edges of flap D and allow it to dry. Lick to activate and press envelope closed to seal. Mmmm good.

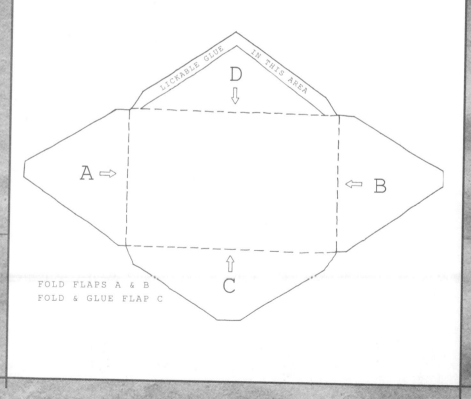

LICKABLE GLUE   IN THIS AREA

D

A ⇨   ⇦ B

FOLD FLAPS A & B
FOLD & GLUE FLAP C   C

Special Gifts

CONCEPTUAL ART REGIFTING

Some of us feel awfully guilty about regifting an unwanted present. We may feel obliged to hang on to the hideous item, be it an atrocious vase or a frightening sweater, even though we hate it. Or at the very least we will lie and say we "bought it especially for you" when we pass along that pretty little selection of jarred marmalade that no one will ever be tempted to eat.

Don't feel bad, feel glad. Regifting is **conceptual art** at its best. All you need is to attach the appropriate label, explaining the "idea," and you've got a work of art of the most high-concept kind, unsullied by laborious process and boring old craftsmanship. Duchamp's notorious urinal-in-an-art-gallery follows this pattern, and in the 1960s numerous artists, including the well-known **Yoko Ono**, made art out of not only objects but also ideas and events. And now so can you.

> **Conceptual Art** An art movement beginning in the 1960s that focuses on art as idea and as exploration, rather than as material object or artifact. Artists of this movement include Joseph Kosuth, Yoko Ono, Douglas Huebler, and Mel Bochner.

> **Yoko Ono** Japanese conceptual artist (b. 1933). Her influential work as part of the Fluxus movement (including performance art such as *Cut Piece*, in which Ono sat passively as audience members participated in cutting her clothes off her body) as well as her experiments with music have been largely overshadowed by her marriage to the "more popular than Jesus" John Lennon of the Beatles.

YOU'LL NEED

An item to regift
Pen and paper to make an explanatory "Label"
A friend with a sense of humor

Take that terrible bowl (Is it a large candy dish? A smallish fruit bowl? A key-and-loose-change receptacle for the hall table?) and attach a label showing the item's provenance—that is, "Purchased and gifted by Great-Aunt Maud on December 25, 2003, to [insert name of appropriate self]. Regifted on December 25, 2004, to [name of lucky recipient] by [name of same self who received the gift last year and appears in the first set of brackets]. Include any and all necessary description of the item and leave space for subsequent regifted names. Provide instructions along the lines of the following: "You are the lucky recipient of a conceptual art gift and are hereby invited to join an artistic regifting process. This item is no longer a mere [insert brief description of item], but an agent of human connection and equalization, allowing the notions of continuity, repetition, and fluid exchange to permeate the holiday season and provide thoughtful contemplation to all and sundry." Or something less high-brow if you prefer, though I find high-brow to be the main point and the source of all the fun with this particular gift idea.

It's especially artful to give something completely inappropriate, like women's clothing to a man or vice versa, as this will prevent the giftee from being tempted to opt out and keep the thing for his or her greedy self. The best part is obviously the practicality, for while it's all quite fun and provides food for thought and all that, it also—let's be honest here—saves you some moolah, as it will mean one less gift for which you actually have to squander cash. This nicely preserves the profound essence of regifting and the Starving Artist's Way. Happy holidays!

ROWS OF DUCKS CANDLES

Raise your hand if you've ever been given creepy Santa or snowman candles at holiday time, only to try to pawn them off on somebody else the following year. Or maybe it's the boring cylindrical ones that pile up in your cabinets. Anyway, there is a never-ending cycle of lame candle collecting that needs breaking. So, let's recycle by doing a little unwanted wax formation transformation. Candles never die, and you might as well give them back in the form of interfaith swimming wax ducks, happily making their merry little way along the edge of the bathtub, for a candlelit evening bathe. It's very Americana—reminiscent both of the classic New England duck-hunt decoy and of cartoony, **Jeff Koons** kitschiness.

Jeff Koons American conceptual/Pop Art sculptor (b. 1955). The 1980s art star and master of kitsch forces the artistic lens to focus on the most banal and goofy of popular culture, from giant porcelain statues of Michael Jackson to "cute" bunnies or puppies cast in metal to glitzy images of Koons himself having sex with his Italian porn-star wife, La Cicciolina. Eventually, Koons eschewed solo art creation and began having his work made, including his paintings, by assistants.

YOU'LL NEED

A rubber ducky or other mold
Matte knife
Piece of gum
Cotton string
Some old candles

Pair of tweezers
Safety gear (gloves, aprons, goggles)
An old, clean coffee can
Old tray or foil-lined bowl

The iconographic rubber ducky itself is your mold, and it will need to be destroyed in the process. Mine came from the 99-cent store and cost, you guessed it, 99 cents—for a family of three—so it's no great financial hardship. If you manage things properly

your duck can create dozens of baby duckling candles for years to come and be well worth the initial investment. Another thing to think about at this juncture is that making a candle out of a rubber ducky will allow you to experience the solid insides of a normally hollow form. OK, so it's not a cast of your entire apartment, but it's still kind of like **Rachel Whiteread** on a teeny tiny scale.

Caution: Hot wax is dangerous, so never leave it unattended and be careful not to spill. Some people choose to wear gloves, aprons, and goggles when handling melted wax, and it is likely that you would be best served by choosing to be some of those people.

First, prepare your ducky for impregnation. Using a matte knife, cut a small, round hole on the very top of the duck's head (you will be

> ## Rachel Whiteread
> English contemporary sculptor (b. 1963), probably most talked of for a plaster cast of the interior of an entire London house.
> Whiteread has also created casts of apartment interiors, a New York City water tower, and other "hollow" spaces complete with all surface detailing displayed in reverse. Whiteread was originally inspired by riffing on Bruce Nauman's one-off piece *A Cast of the Space Under My Chair* (1965-68). Whiteread made several of these forms, moving eventually onto the undersides of tables and beyond.

pouring wax through here, so don't make it too tiny—nickel size is good). Cut a slit from this hole straight down the back of the duck's head and down the back to the tip of the tail. Cut perpendicularly across from wing to wing as if you are giving your duck an emergency C-section from behind (see drawing). All this cutting is so you will be able to remove the finished candle after it has cooled. Plus, slicing things in half is likely to make you feel as bold as **Gordon Matta-Clark,** so what could be bad?

Gordon Matta-Clark   American multimedia artist/architect (1943–1978) who became famous for slicing buildings down the middle with a chainsaw, creating slivers of air and light that extended entirely through the structures. He died from cancer at the startlingly young age of 35.

Take a couple of pieces of chewed bubble gum (if you don't want to chew it, or it's already gone hard, you can knead it for a few minutes under warm running water to rinse the sugar and flavoring away and to make it pliable) and press the gum over the crisscrossing cuts on the outside of the duck to seal them shut, leaving only the hole open at the top of the duck's head. Press firmly. Also, push a bit of gum into the air hole on the duck's belly to seal that and set him into a foil-lined baking tray or into an aluminum take-out tray in case wax spills over his sides or he springs an unexpected leak. (Notice the anthropomorphizing of the inanimate rubber ducky implied by the use of the word *him*. This is a perfectly normal and entertaining bit of goofiness. Don't bother to fight it.)

Take a wick (either an ordinary bit of cotton string or a wick salvaged with tweezers from one of your melting candles) and poke it down through the head opening and into the body so it rests on the duck-belly floor. Stick the protruding wick end to some gum just outside the opening, so it stays upright and you don't have to hold it in place.

Melt the ugly or unwanted candles in a coffee can set into a pot of boiling water. Melt the wax about three-fourths of the way and then turn off the heat and stir the candles, allowing the heat of the melted wax to soften the rest. You want it to become uniformly liquid, but you don't want it to start to cook or to get too hot.

Carefully pour the melted wax into the body of the duck. If some spills over the side, just let it run into the tray and don't worry about it. You can salvage this wax for use on the next candle after it's cooled. Fill the duck to the opening and then just let it cool in a place where it won't get knocked over. You will notice that the wax will settle a bit as it hardens, leaving a gap at the top. You will subsequently add more melted wax and allow it to harden again. Repeat until the mold is filled. This is just basic casting, which on a larger scale gives you such memorable and oft recast works of art as **Rodin**'s *The Thinker*.

If your mold leaks, just stop pouring and let the wax cool and harden. When the wax has solidified you can reseal

Auguste Rodin French sculptor (1840–1917) famous for his realist portraits, such as *The Thinker* (1880) and *The Kiss* (1006), both originally cast in bronze, though recasts of both are so numerous worldwide as to qualify as cliché.

the leaky spot with more gum, and reuse any wax that ran out into the tray. Then try, try again.

Allow the duck to cool. When Monsieur Duckling is cool and firm to the touch (give it a couple of hours), you can remove the gum and gently pull the mold open to push out the candle.

Repeat as necessary until you have a row of four or five ducks. Even if they are imperfect with rough spots or flat areas on the tops of their heads from the pour hole, they will still look like a row of ducks and they will still be fun. Repetition makes it easy to forgive imperfections.

Of course anything can be a candle mold if it won't melt from proximity to hot wax and if you can get the candle out of it in the end. Figure out your own surgery diagrams for other rubber items, as well as plastic doll heads and anything else you can think of.

ARTFUL PHOTO ALBUMS

When you lay out a photo album, you might consider labeling the pictures with high-falutin' names, fortunes saved from fortune cookies, or newspaper headlines chosen at random. Everyone will get a laugh out of a photo album with an extra touch of wit and style.

Photos can be "defined" to enhance their inherent drama and entertainment value. Pictures of a class or family reunion with the headline "Peace Talks Under Way in the Middle East" might amuse you for years to come. Try naming your trip pix as if you'd been on a grand adventure. **Richard Long** did the flip side of this idea, walking around as art and then documenting it with photos such as *A Six Day Walk Over All Roads, Lanes and Double Tracks Inside a Six Mile Wide Circle Centered on the Giant Cerne Abbas* (1975). You can use long names like that or even just name some of them "Untitled Still" in a smart-ass tribute to **Cindy Sherman.** Try thinking of your life and activities as experiments in art-making and your photos as the proof. Consider creating something like **Douglas Huebler**'s *Site Sculpture Project, 50 Mile Piece, Haverhill, Mass.–Putney, Vt.–New York City* (1968), which is, you guessed it, his photos of a long drive. I'm sure you've taken a long drive or two of your own. Did you know it was art?

Richard Long English environmental artist (b. 1945) who uses walking as a medium for making art, which he then records with maps, photos, or writing. Although he also creates physical sculptures out of rocks, sticks, and other natural, found materials, Long posits that his footprints, and even his untraceable passage through a landscape, are sculpture, too. Basically, the point is that taking a walk, even if nobody ever knows about it, is a work of art.

Cindy Sherman American Post-Modern photographer (b. 1954). She has made a career of photographing herself, most famously for her *Untitled Film Stills* (1977–80), a series of self-portraits with Sherman cast in a variety of traditionally forgettable female roles from nonexistent B-movies, the real twist being, that in this case she is also the "artist."

Douglas Huebler American conceptual artist (1924–1997) who created photographic narratives, using the photo image as a medium to explore process.

OUT-OF-FOCUS PHOTO ALBUM

Sadly, with the advent of all this foolproof digital technology, we lose a little touch of mystery every day. Auto-focus has its advantages, like sparing us from the standing-around-while-the-photographer-gets-things-together   part of life, though pro photographers have generally continued to use manual adjustments anyway because it provides more options. Maybe you want to focus on that one little raindrop right there and blur out the rest of the jungle.... Whatever these considerations might be, there are those of us who still generate the occasional out-of-focus or badly exposed photo, often because we don't understand our cameras all that well. Are these outtakes garbage? Oh, no. These are the masterpieces of the art world. Ask the crowds swarming to admire the soft-focus black-and-white imagery of **Gerhard Richter,** the darling of late-twentieth-century painting.

> **Gerhard Richter**
> German Neo-Expressionist painter (b. 1932) who is strangely like two painters. With some of his time he creates huge and colorful, abstract squeegee paintings. Otherwise he's occupied by black-and-white painted copies of photographs blurred into soft focus, famously those of the Baader-Meinhof group of jailed German activists-turned-terrorists.

YOU'LL NEED
Photo album and photos
Label and pen

Your "failed" photos deserve a special presentation all their own. Something that happens one time can appear to be a mistake, but if you manage to collect 20 or 30 of these babies, no one will try to deny that you've created a work of art. Look at **Nan Goldin**'s photos of her friends all hanging out in the '80s. One of those on their own might look no more like a work of art than *your* photos of *your* friends—but a whole book-full—now that shows *intent,* which is basically the frame that distinguishes art from everything else.

Nan Goldin American photographer (b. 1953) who chronicled the era of AIDS in downtown New York City. Her photos are gritty and glaring "snapshots" of the people around her hanging out, making out, shooting up, and doing all kinds of other edgy and/or ordinary stuff.

You might alternately try the "red-eye vampire" photo album or the "under/over exposed worlds-of-light-and-darkness" albums, as these types of photos are still being produced by the dozens out of even the latest, expensive cameras. Just clearly label your album with letters on the cover, as embracing and renaming what others would call a fiasco is the whole game.

Or if you have an archive of bad photos spanning generations, you might try "The Eyes Wide Shut Holiday Picture Book" or the "Headless Family Gatherings Photos." These are popular gifts and as works of art they explore themes of redemption and acceptance. Kind of like the religious paintings of the Renaissance.

EXISTENTIAL POETRY BOOKS

Collage artist Kathy Bruce contributed this quirky idea, something she created as a gift for her son, to give him something more philosophical to think about than what children's reading usually provides.

The words in these books are all cutouts, as you might expect from a collage artist, and their look is reminiscent of a **Barbara Kruger** poster. Kathy strings together nouns and verbs that look interesting to her and crafts short poems. She then laminates the pages at a copy shop and binds them into books with a three-hole punch and some binder rings.

Existentialism A philosophical movement dealing with issues of the individual's responsibility in an incomprehensible universe and the notion that you are defined by what you choose to do. Famous existentialists are Søren Kierkegaard, Friedrich Nietzsche, Jean-Paul Sartre, Simone de Beauvoir, and Albert Camus.

Barbara Kruger American conceptual artist (b. 1945) who creates propagandistic posters using slogany text over found imagery in a red, black, and white color scheme to explore the power of media control, as well as to exert that self-same influence in support of her chosen political ideas.

YOU'LL NEED

Words on paper (old books, greeting cards, or periodicals)
Scissors and glue stick

Kathy uses large-print words from old kids' books or scientific texts. If you can't find large text, do the following: Cut out your chosen source words that will form the poem and glue them with glue stick to a sheet of typing paper. Blow this up to 200 percent or more on a color copier (to preserve the colors of the letters and backgrounds), and cut them out again. This way you'll have nice large words and you will even be able to cull them from among the smaller areas of text. Stick the words onto a sheet of colored paper in poem formation.

If you can afford the copy shop bill, it's nice to recopy this page so that the final poem is permanent and the words are smooth on the surface of the page. Some tips from Kathy: older books often have old-fashioned, different words, and you won't feel as guilty about cutting them up. Think about how the word looks and how it is arranged on the page, as well as the meaning.

You could do a book of five to ten poems with the same 20 words rearranged for each one. In a pinch, old greeting card texts are nice to rearrange for this; for example, "Graduation to Your Congratulations on You" sounds pretty deep.

CHAPTER SIXTEEN

Festive Edibles

PAUL KLEE EDIBLE MOSAIC CAKE

L et's face it, the reason we don't decorate cakes at home is because it's just too hard. It's horribly messy dealing with all that gooey, oozing icing and trying to actually draw something with a bulging, sticky icing bag that won't come out looking like one of those squishy **Claes Oldenburg** cake-sculptures is an exercise in utter frustration.

Enter gum paste, the foolproof solution to decorating a special-occasion cake. Gum paste is a sugary dough that you can buy at any good cake supply store (i.e., New York Cake and Baking Distributors, 56 W. 26 Street, New York, NY 10011, or order by phone: 212-675-2253). The paste is naturally white, but you can mix up small amounts of different colors using ordinary food coloring and then you've got a basic Play-Doh situation. If you are really good with your hands, you can make tiny sculptural objects or figurines out of the stuff. Or you

Claes Oldenburg
Swedish-born American Pop artist (b. 1929). He is most famous for giant "soft" sculptures, made from cloth or vinyl, representing various foods, appliances, and ordinary objects, such as burgers, slices of pie, and a fan. Since the 1970s, he has collaborated with his wife and fellow artist, Coosje Van Bruggen, on large-scale architectural works.

can make flowers by forming oval petals and draping them over the back of a spoon until they harden into curves, which you can then stick onto the iced cake. The icing will act like glue.

YOU'LL NEED

Iced cake

Gum paste

Food coloring

knife and rolling pin (or the side of a clean wine bottle for rolling)

One of my favorite and easiest cake-decorating design ideas is to make small squares of several different shades of one color. Mix small bunches and add one extra drop of food coloring to each until you have about ten different hues, and then roll them out and cut squares with a knife. When you lay the squares side by side around the edges or sides of the cake, allowing different shades to lie next to each other, they create a mosaic effect like a **Paul Klee** painting. Tint the color of the base icing first, so you won't have to fill every inch. Use pale blues, purples, and greens for a beautiful effect.

Paul Klee Swiss Expressionist painter (1879–1940). Member of Der Blaue Reiter, an Expressionist group of the early twentieth century who taught at the Bauhaus along with Wassily Kandinsky and explored themes of metaphysics, transcendentalism, and the primitive. He is hard to classify, having connections with both Surrealism and Cubism, and he used symbols and signs in an attempt to access the "reality that is behind visible things." He is one of those artists who were termed "degenerate" by the Nazis, a label that has, for obvious reasons, turned out to be something of a compliment.

FORTUNE COOKIES

Somebody suggested to me that if I marketed a line of fortune cookies that actually tasted good, I would make a killing. I'm sure that's true. What's not to love about cookies with secret messages inside that are also mighty tasty? However, as I'm a Starving Artist and not an entrepreneur, I guess I'll have to leave it to some business mogul to rip off my idea and get rich with fortune cookies that are more than just a novelty item and have that *je ne sais quoi* of actual deliciousness.

The fortunes you use here can be anything, of course. you can copy some **Jenny Holzer** "truisms" onto slips of paper. Some examples are "eating too much is criminal," "fake or real indifference is a powerful personal weapon," and the

> **Jenny Holzer** American graphic/installation artist (b. 1950) who gained prominence with her authoritative statements disseminated via posters and the uncommon artistic medium of LCD displays.

particularly memorable "lack of charisma can be fatal." They are more provocative, but otherwise similar to the "unfortunes" you usually get in the smart-aleck cookies, which don't actually tell you anything about the future, but just announce something inscrutable about who you are or how the world works. You can go equally esoteric with random strips of text cut from magazines.

Usually fortune cookie recipes use just egg whites, leaving the yolks to go to waste. Wastefulness is not the way of the Starving Artist, however, so use the whole eggs unless you have a pre-existing plan for solo yolks. Yolks also make the cookies taste better.

Make your fortunes first, on colored strips of paper about 2½ inches long by ¼ inch wide. Write whatever you want. You can't go wrong with some **e. e. cummings** first lines, including "nobody loses all the time" or "all which isn't singing is mere talking." Or even any sentence out of **Allen Ginsberg**'s *America*—"I can't stand my own mind" or the slightly dated but still amusing "America it's them bad Russians." Fold in half the long way to protect the text when it goes into the warm cookie.

> ### e. e. cummings
> American Modernist poet (1894–1962) who shunned the use of capital letters including for the spelling of his own name, correctly written above. An uncommonly popular poet, cummings generally spent half his day painting or drawing and half writing poetry.

The following recipe is for an almond-lemon cookie, softer and tastier than the Chinese restaurant type. Feel free to swap out the lemon and almond for a tablespoon or two of some cocoa powder or instant coffee mixed with a tablespoon of water, or a shot of a tasty liqueur.

Allen Ginsberg American Beat poet (1926–1997) and pal of William S. Burroughs and Jack Kerouac, as well as author of *Howl* (1955), the epic poem that launched the Beat movement. He grew up in Paterson, New Jersey, the town immortalized by poet William Carlos Williams, and went on to become one of the most famous poets of the twentieth century.

YOU'LL NEED

1/3 cup sugar	3 tablespoons butter, melted
1/2 cup all-purpose flour	2 eggs
1/2 teaspoon salt	3 tablespoons cream or milk
1 teaspoon cornstarch	1 teaspoon vanilla extract
1/4 cup ground almonds	Juice of 1 lemon

Preheat the oven to 400 degrees. Mix the dry ingredients in a bowl. Whisk in the remaining ingredients.

Put a tablespoon of the batter onto a greased sheet of foil on a baking sheet. Spread the batter outward with the spoon until it forms a large, thin circle approximately 4 or 5 inches in diameter. Make one or two additional cookies, making sure to leave a couple of inches between each one so they won't run together. Bake about 10 minutes or until the cookies are brown on the edges, and then remove them from the oven.

Immediately remove the first cookie with a spatula and place on a cloth napkin. Lay the fortune across it and fold the cookie in half over the fortune, pressing the center of the semicircular edges together for 3 or 4 seconds. Fold in half again and press in the center again. Put aside and repeat the procedure with the other already-baked cookies before they cool and harden. Then, bake the next batch. Leave the cookies to set so they have a touch of crunchiness before they get eaten.

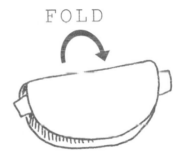

FOLD

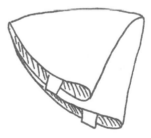

Note: The form given here is different from that of a traditional fortune cookie because it is tricky for those of us with limited time to work the cookies into that shape without wasting half of them. If you aren't into baking, you can get store-bought fortune cookies, steam them lightly to soften, and then unfold. Replace with your own fortunes, refold, and allow them to cool and harden.

THREE-TIERED CAKE

My friend Will von Hartz taught me how to make an extremely fancy tiered cake for another friend's wedding. He didn't invent this process, but he's been obsessed with cake-making for years and has learned all the good tricks. The tough part is that you need three different size double cakes for the three tiers (each double cake is a layer attached to another of the same size with a swath of icing), but if you can't manage getting a hold of the three different sizes of round pans, you can bake them all the same largest size and then cut down four of them to make the two smaller tiers by tracing something round, like a large can or plate. You'll waste some cake that way, but it means you'll have some for sampling, so that's not really a problem at all. You can also buy different size cakes from a bakery and reconfigure them yourself, which will allow you control of the design and save some money.

YOU'LL NEED

6 round cakes baked according to your favorite recipe (2 of each size: small, medium, and large)

Icing of your choice

Cardboard

A pencil

Scissors

2 dozen plastic drinking straws

A yard or two of ribbon

A few straight pins

For each of the two smaller rounds, place the cake on a sheet of cardboard and trace around. Cut out so you have a cardboard disk the exact size of the tier that will fit it perfectly. Place the largest rounds on a serving tray or plate, stacking the two layers into a double layer cake and icing it. Ice the other double tiers on their cardboard rounds. Allow the cakes to set in the refrigerator so the icing's fairly durable.

Now comes the **Mies van der Rohe** moment: you are going to build a support structure able to bear vertical weight and buoy the tower of cake. Gently place the second level, centered, on the first. With a straight pin, quickly trace around the base of the second tier onto the first and then remove the tier. If you leave it for too long your cake can begin to sag and collapse.

Ludwig Mies van der Rohe

German Modernist architect (1886–1969), former director of the Bauhaus, and one of the most famous builders of American classic skyscrapers. Generally referred to simply as "Mies" (pronounced "meez"), he was one of the primary innovators of what became known as the Chicago Style. With protégé Philip Johnson, he designed New York's Seagram Building and he would have appreciated my keeping this blurb short: his famously succinct motto was "less is more."

Take a plastic drinking straw and plunge it into the center of the base layer, straight upright until it won't go any further. Mark the exact point where it emerges from the cake. Pull it out and cut it there with a pair of scissors, so that you have a straw the exact height of your cake. Cut five more identical straws. Put the one back in the center, and the other five in a circle around it, just inside the ring you've traced onto the cake's surface. They should reach right to the surface of the cake and no further.

Now, place your second tier back onto the marked circle, covering this support structure. Follow the same procedure for the next layer. If the cardboard rounds show under the base of the tiers, you can wrap a ribbon around the base, covering it, and pin the ribbon in back of the cake with a bead head pin.

Put some decorative flowers or more icing into the spots on the cake you may have smudged when moving the layers around. Or just cover the cake with candy like a gingerbread-style **Will Cotton** candy house. Ornament is no crime, in spite of what **Adolf Loos** might say on the subject.

> **Will Cotton** American contemporary painter (b. 1965). Creator of slickly enticing paintings of candy, cakes, and the combination of the two in the form of carefully constructed confectionary houses.

Don't forget to remove the pins and straws before cutting. You'll want to dismantle the layers for cutting after everyone's gotten a good long look at your masterpiece.

> **Adolf Loos** Austrian Modernist architect and critic (1870–1933) whose horror of all things old-fashioned, decadent, or kitschy led him to pen the 1908 essay "Ornament and Crime," in which he decries the use of meaningless decoration.

Decorative Extras

STARBURSTS: TOOTHPICKS AND ASSORTED HARDWARE

Toothpicks are among the most versatile of the Starving Artist's tools. The question here should really be, "What can't you make out of toothpicks?" and then I would write a short list of a dozen or so items and be done with this segment and on to the next one. Instead, I'll attempt to choose the simplest and most rewarding of toothpick projects. I won't, for example, suggest that you try a remake of **Ann Hamilton**'s *Toothpick Suit*— that is impractical. That would be *hard*.

> **Ann Hamilton** American installation artist (b. 1956) who made a wearable *Toothpick Suit* and has created pieces from textiles, Braille-embossed walls, candies, and turkey carcasses, her pieces usually including a display of obsessive-compulsive labor and multiplicity: did I mention the *Toothpick Suit*?

A no-skills but striking piece is the toothpick starburst, an appealing porcupine-like decorative item reminiscent of Tom Friedman's (see page 191) toothpick sculpture. The starburst is great as a holiday ornament or in a bowl as an arty update to the dish of seashells. Think of it as the twenty-first-century version of the "orange-with-the-cloves-stuck-in-it" crafted ornaments of the olden days. The starburst can also be dusted with a light coating of spray paint if you want to transform it into something more mysterious or more glam.

If his opinion were asked, **Lucas Samaras** would probably make these starbursts out of small nails or other hardware instead of toothpicks, and the resulting orb becomes less like an obscure sea urchin and more like a postapocalyptic, tiny armored vehicle in which a futuristic warrior sea creature might ride to do battle with the aforementioned sea urchin. They are very impressive.

> **Lucas Samaras** Greek-born American photographer, painter, and assemblage artist (b. 1936) who, while incredibly prolific in all his chosen media, is best known for his circa 1970s series of altered "Autopolaroid" self-portrait photographs. Samaras is also known for his sculptural jewelry boxes encrusted with nail-and-pin jewels, stripes and spirals of yarn, and all kinds of other found objects.

YOU'LL NEED

A Styrofoam ball

1,000–2,000 round (as opposed to flat) toothpicks, which will probably be several boxes, depending on how many you find per box

or

A few hundred straight pins, small nails, screws, thumbtacks, etc., for the industrial variation

Thread and a pin (optional)

Get a small-size Styrofoam ball from a craft or plastics store. A manageable size would be 2½ inches or smaller. If you will want to hang this ball you'll need first of all to tie some thread or fishing line to a pin and embed the pin in the Styrofoam up to its head. Now you have a string hanging off—leave it about 12 inches long for now—you can always cut it later. If you want to color the ball itself, so the tiny bits that show between the spikes are prettier, coat the ball first with white glue. Then you can give it a dusting of spray paint. Without the glue the spray paint will dissolve the Styrofoam.

Next, start sticking the toothpicks (or nails) into the Styrofoam ball. Work circularly from one point outward so you have room to get your hand in. You need to embed the sticks only about ⅛ inch or so. Press them as long as they go easily. They'll resist you at the point where they widen, and that's a good point to stop forcing it. Keep the picks close together, as you don't want too much scalp to show between them, and keep at it till you cover the entire sphere. When you've filled most of the ball, you might find it easiest to work by resting the starburst on a cushion on your lap, to avoid getting pricked by its urchin-y exterior. Don't stress about getting the spikes to exactly the same depth. If some stick out more than others, it will look great anyway.

ZODIAC DECAL DINNER PARTY NAPKINS

If you've got a dinner party planned and you want to entertain like a Starving Artist, you'll need a set of cloth napkins. For one thing, they are reusable, which saves money. For another thing, cloth napkins are what you get in nice restaurants, so it makes people feel taken care of, which will make them want to come over for more dinner parties, making you extremely popular. These will also make a good wedding gift. Old napkins from the thrift store are beautiful and extremely inexpensive, because people discard sets of napkins as soon as one is ruined. Too bad for them; it's surely not our problem if they can't think of a better solution for mismatched napkins than the trash.

Zodiac napkins are fun because it gives people something to talk about as soon as they sit at the table—watch them try to name the symbols, jockey to sit at their own sign, or trade napkins with one another. Obviously, you don't have to use all 12 signs at once if you have fewer people—just pick and choose or put out the stack and let your guests choose for themselves. You can set some empty place settings if you like, for conspicuously missing people of your choice, and raise controversial discussions about those not invited to or missing from the table in homage to **Judy Chicago**'s *The Dinner Party* or **Karen Finley**'s *The Vacant Chair*.

> **Judy Chicago**   American installation artist (b. 1939) and feminist whose classic 1970s piece *The Dinner Party* established her name. The piece incorporated the craft media of needlework and ceramics and was a giant triangular banquet table with chronological place settings for important women in history.

> **Karen Finley**   American performance artist (b. 1956) who was one of the artists branded "indecent," provoking the NEA uproar of the 1980s. While the vitriol against her at that time focused on her smearing chocolate over her naked body, she has worked in wide-ranging media including recording poetry rants, acting, and writing books, including the satirical *Living It Up: Humorous Adventures in Hyperdomesticity*, which parodies Martha Stewart and lifestyle books more or less like this one.

YOU'LL NEED

12 cloth napkins

Iron-on transfer paper

Computer with a printer or access to a copy shop

Scissors

Iron

Find cloth napkins of assorted shapes and sizes at a thrift store. Each napkin will be different, but the images will *tie* them *in* and make them clearly "a set." The Wingdings font has all 12 zodiac symbols, which you can enlarge to the appropriate size (at least 72 point), turn into whatever color you like on a computer, and print onto iron-on paper from the stationery store. If you like, you can browse online for zodiac symbols and print them. Make sure, however, that you reverse the nonsymmetrical images before printing, so they will read correctly when ironed on. Then, carefully cut out the image and iron one symbol onto

the front face of each napkin. You should use a hot iron without steam and press firmly in a circular motion for about 60 seconds.

Or, if you don't have a computer or printer, have the illustrations (page 263) blown up and copied at your local copy shop, and make the decals from there. You can also use the symbols to make stencils or mini silkscreens (see silkscreen T-shirt instructions on page 177).

NEW YEAR'S TRASH HATS

Bored of the same old New Year's Eve plans? No doubt. Try this project and you can earn a reputation for being the life of the party. Filmmaker/animator Ellie Lee offered this crafty, good idea, something she learned from her artist friend Sean Daly. Sean developed it out of postholiday junk as a way to dress up for "first night" in Boston. The idea is to make New Year's hats out of "trash," as Ellie describes it. Wearing some of the hats themselves, the friends also bring along a bag full of extra hats to give out at the parties. That's not only bringing along the fun, it's almost like **performance art**—or you can imagine yourself a **Fluxus** artist.

> **Performance Art**   The idea of art as a live event, rather than as object, first used in the early 1960s to describe Happenings, Fluxus, and Actionism. Vito Acconci, Marina Abramovic, Yoko Ono, Laurie Anderson, Karen Finley, and Mariko Mori are all, at least some of the time, performance artists.

> **Fluxus**   An art movement beginning in the early 1960s, with connections to Dadaism and characterized by often humorous radicalism in the realms of performance art and music. Events were referred to as "Aktions" or "Happenings," and artists involved include Nam June Paik, Yoko Ono, John Cage, and Joseph Beuys.

YOU'LL NEED

Newspaper and leftover wrapping paper and bows
Scotch tape

The basic hat shape is the cone. This is pretty festive as it looks like a magician's hat or one of the princess cone-crowns from the Middle Ages. It's also supremely easy. Roll a double thickness of newspaper into a cone and use Scotch tape to hold the shape. Trim the bottom edge to a straight line. If you want to add strings to hold it more securely on your head, you can staple a couple onto the brim about where your ears are and tie them under your chin.

Try making any of the hats from the templates in this book. They can be cut out of stiff paper or cardboard and put together with tape.

Cut a long strip of ½-inch-wide paper, curl it around a pencil, and press for a second to hold the shape. Cut vertically down the middle, turn the two curls back to back, and staple them to the point of your hat so they cascade down with a flourish.

Crush balls of bright paper and tape them onto your hat. Cut out stars, butterflies, etc., from magazines and glue them on. These hats should be quick and bright, not finicky and perfect. Leftover bows and other wrappings from the winter holidays can be taped onto the hats.

Fill a clear recycling bag with the spare hats so that people you meet can ask you why you're carrying them. Shake confetti and glitter into the bag so that there's more commotion when you pull the hats out. Give all the hats away before the night is through, for maximum fun. Wear the crushed remains to breakfast and then toss them into the recycling bag and leave by the curb in the morning.

Useful Info
Some Definitions

Grommet   A front-and-back pair of metal rings that you jam onto fabric to support a hole (like an instant, super-strong button hole).

Decoupage   Decorative bits of paper glued onto other surfaces and then coated with a sealant.

Stencil   A cut-out design in negative that you paint through to create a positive image.

Spray mount   Toxic spray glue best used outdoors, but perfect for gluing paper smoothly without any wetness or peeling off.

Hot glue   Rubbery tubes that melt in a gun-like dispenser and work well for quick-drying, short-term bonds. Though you could burn yourself if you aren't careful, hot glue is not particularly toxic.

Wood glue   The glue used by carpenters, which makes an extremely strong bond with woods and papers. Behaves just like white glue, except for the yellowish color. No fumes.

Precision/hobby knife   The same as X-Acto (which, like Kleenex, is a brand name that has become the most common name for the thing itself), basically a hand-held blade for cutting very neatly.

Craft/utility/matte knife   Like the knife above, but bigger and sturdier for less precise and often grungier jobs.

Kraft paper   Sturdy paper (usually brown) most often used for protecting work surfaces.

Some Things to Know

Check out the website www.thistothat.com for gluing solutions if you don't know what kind to use.

If you are doing a lot of sewing with heavy fabric or leather, a thimble will keep your finger from hurting where you push the needle through. A thimble cuts down on flexibility of movement, however, so try wrapping the tip of your thimble finger with masking tape for a protective, thick skin.

You can speed up the process of paint drying with a hairdryer or a well-placed fan.

Use a straightedge to make straight edges! Besides a ruler, this can be anything straight in your house, though it should be metal if you are planning to cut along its edge. Try a tool box or a kitchen bread box.

Keep the blades sharp in your hobby or utility knives (no, don't sharpen them—replace them often). Accuracy and ease are inversely affected by a crappy, overused blade.

When screwing into metal, make an indentation where you intend to screw by using a hammer and nail. The small dent you make will keep the drill from skidding all over the slick surface when you start.

When screwing into Sheetrock walls, use a butterfly, also known as anchor, toggle bolt, or toggler (depending on whom you ask) to support your screw. This goes into the wall first and prevents the screw from ripping out of the plaster board. It's an alternative to finding a stud to screw into. However, if your sheetrock is less than ⅝ inches thick, or old or damp, you *must* find a stud for your screw—the butter-flanchgler bolt won't help you.

Spray glues are pretty versatile and can be used even for small items. You can spray some into a bottle cap and use a Q-tip to apply the glue to a controlled area.

If you use a cordless screw gun, make sure the battery is properly charged or the job will be unnecessarily hard. Keep the spare battery charging while you work.

Use shampoo to clean fine washables. The Starving Artist doesn't need to muck around with high-priced dry cleaning technology. Those chemicals cause cancer anyway. Soak sweater and other deli-cates for a couple of hours in a cold sink-bath with a touch of sham-poo (think about it—it's delicate enough for your hair). Rinse cold, gently press out excess water without wringing, and dry flat on a towel.

Make natural dyes of coffee, tea, beets, onion skins, turmeric, and Kool-Aid. Use them to color fabrics, Easter eggs, or whatever else. The coffees and teas are brown and beige, the beets are purple, and the onion skins and turmeric are yellow. Most Kool-Aid flavors turn things some shade of pink or purple and also provide an artificial fruity smell, which may or may not appeal to you. As with any dye, just mix it up by adding it to boiling water and give it time to dissolve and deeply color the water. Best colors result from keeping the dye bath hot on the stove while your item soaks. The color of the dye bath should be substantially deeper than the desired shade as all dyes rinse out to some degree, leaving a softer, paler color when finished.

Baking soda will clean almost anything and it prevents odors, too. Sprinkle on to dirt and rust and rub with a damp cloth. Mix with dishwashing soap to make a paste for scrubbing kitchens and bathrooms. Mix with vinegar to clean rust. Mix with 3 percent hydrogen peroxide to naturally clean your teeth. There are no limits.

Some Things to Save

Be a pack rat. Save wrappings and packaging, brightly colored bags, strings, ribbons and paper, cards or scraps of magazines with cool imagery, labels, tags, empty cosmetics containers (that you like), nice old keys, ball bearings and other special bits of metal or machine parts, nice rocks, or bits of glass. Cut trimming and buttons off clothing that you intend to throw away.

Bibliography

Anderson, Maxwell Lincoln, ed. *Whitney Biennial: 2000 Exhibition.* New York: Whitney Museum of Art, 2002.

Archer, Michael. *Art Since 1960.* New York: Thames & Hudson, 2002.

Barron, Stephanie, and Lynn Zelevansky. *Jasper Johns to Jeff Koons: Four Decades of Art from the Broad Collection.* Los Angeles: Los Angeles County Museum of Art; New York: In association with H.N. Abrams, 2001.

Berthold-Bond, Annie. *Better Basics for the Home.* New York: Three Rivers Press, 1999.

Clark, Linda. *Secrets of Health & Beauty.* New York: Pyramid Books, 1975.

De Chassey, Eric, ed. *American Art 1908–1947: From Winslow Homer to Jackson Pollock.* Paris: Éditions de la Réunion des Musées Nationaux; New York: Harry N. Abrams, 2002.

Diehl, Carol. "Mix-Master." *Art in America,* September 2003.

Flam, Jack, ed. *Robert Smithson: The Complete Writings.* Berkeley: University of California Press, 1996.

Heartney, Eleanor. "An Art of Tender Recuperation." *Art in America,* July 2003.

Henry, Hugues. "Let's pie! Let's pie! Nincompoop guys! *The Netly News,* February 9, 1998.

Hoffman, Abbie; co-conspirator, Izak Haber; accessory after the fact, Bert Cohen. *Steal This Book.* New York: Pirate Editions; distributed by Grove Press, 1971.

Janson, H. W., and Anthony F. Janson. *History of Art.* New York: Harry N. Abrams, 1991.

Koether, Jutta. "Interview with Martin Kippenberger." *Flash Art,* Jan/Feb 1990.

Malcolm, Janet. *The Purloined Clinic: Selected Writings.* New York: Vintage Books, 1993.

Mish, Frederick C., ed. *Webster's Ninth New Collegiate Dictionary.* Springfield: Merriam-Webster Inc., 1991.

Rand, Harry. *Hundertwasser.* Cologne. Benedikt Taschen, 1991.

Rubinstein, Charlotte Streifer. *American Women Artists: From Early Indian Times to the Present.* New York: Avon; Boston: G.K. Hall, 1982.

Schellmann, Jörg, ed. *Joseph Beuys, the multiples: catalogue raisonné of multiples and prints.* Cambridge: Busch-Reisings Museum, Harvard University Museum; Minneapolis: Walker Art Center; Munich; New York: Edition Schellmann, 1997.

Vergo, Peter. *Art in Vienna 1898–1918.* Oxford: Phaidon Press Limited, 1975.

Index